SandCastle

Sight Words

Was That Fun?

Kelly Doudna

Consulting Editor Monica Marx, M.A./Reading Specialist

ABDO
Publishing Company

Published by SandCastle™, an imprint of ABDO Publishing Company, 4940 Viking Drive, Edina, Minnesota 55435.

Printed in the United States.

Credits
Edited by: Pam Price
Curriculum Coordinator: Nancy Tuminelly
Cover and Interior Design and Production: Mighty Media
Photo Credits: BananaStock Ltd., Comstock, Corbis Images, PhotoDisc, Stockbyte

Library of Congress Cataloging-in-Publication Data

Doudna, Kelly, 1963-
    Was that fun? / Kelly Doudna.
        p. cm. -- (Sight words)
    Includes index.
    Summary: Uses simple sentences, photographs, and a brief story to introduce six different words: after, been, have, so, to, was.
    ISBN 1-59197-475-5
    1. Readers (Primary) 2. Vocabulary--Juvenile literature. [1. Reading.] I. Title. II. Series.

PE1119.D68664 2003
428.1--dc21

                                                                        2003050324

SandCastle™ books are created by a professional team of educators, reading specialists, and content developers around five essential components that include phonemic awareness, phonics, vocabulary, text comprehension, and fluency. All books are written, reviewed, and leveled for guided reading, early intervention reading, and Accelerated Reader® programs and designed for use in shared, guided, and independent reading and writing activities to support a balanced approach to literacy instruction.

Let Us Know

After reading the book, SandCastle would like you to tell us your stories about reading. What is your favorite page? Was there something hard that you needed help with? Share the ups and downs of learning to read. We want to hear from you! To get posted on the ABDO Publishing Company Web site, send us e-mail at:

sandcastle@abdopub.com

SandCastle Level: Beginning

Featured Sight Words

after   been

have   so

to   was

Sam wraps up in a towel after he swims.

Max and Liz have been at the beach all day.

The kids have green
and purple noodles.

Jo has so much fun swimming.

Kim takes her pink inner tube to the pool.

Dave was at the pool with his parents.

The Beach
Was Fun

The Smiths have been at the beach.

They like to go often.

They chase after each other.

The water feels so good.

It was sunny.

They have had fun.

More Sight Words in This Book

a	had	like
all	has	much
and	he	other
at	her	the
day	his	they
go	in	up
good	it	with

All words identified as sight words in this book are from Edward Bernard Fry's "First Hundred Instant Sight Words."

Picture Index

beach, pp. 7, 16

green, p. 9

pink, p. 13

pool, pp. 13, 15

purple, p. 9

towel, p. 5

About SandCastle™

A professional team of educators, reading specialists, and content developers created the SandCastle™ series to support young readers as they develop reading skills and strategies and increase their general knowledge. The SandCastle™ series has four levels that correspond to early literacy development in young children. The levels are provided to help teachers and parents select the appropriate books for young readers.

Emerging Readers
(no flags)

Beginning Readers
(1 flag)

Transitional Readers
(2 flags)

Fluent Readers
(3 flags)

These levels are meant only as a guide. All levels are subject to change.

To see a complete list of SandCastle™ books and other nonfiction titles from ABDO Publishing Company, visit **www.abdopub.com** or contact us at:

4940 Viking Drive, Edina, Minnesota 55435 • 1-800-800-1312 • fax: 1-952-831-1632

Fifty Fables of La Fontaine

Fifty Fables *of* La Fontaine

ॐ

Translated by
Norman R. Shapiro

with illustrations by
Alan James Robinson

University of Illinois Press
Urbana and Chicago

© 1985, 1988 by Norman R. Shapiro
Illustrations © 1988 by Alan James Robinson
Manufactured in the United States of America
C 5 4 3 2 1

This book is printed on acid-free paper.

Library of Congress Cataloging-in-Publication Data

La Fontaine, Jean de, 1621–1695.
  [Fables. English. Selections]
  Fifty fables of La Fontaine / translated by Norman R. Shapiro;
with illustrations by Alan James Robinson.
    p.   cm.
  ISBN 0-252-01513-4 (alk. paper)
    1. Fables. French—Translations into English. 2. Fables, English-
-Translations from French. I. Shapiro, Norman R. II. Title.
PQ1811.E3S45 1988
841'.4—dc19   87-28750
                                                        CIP

For Evelyn

CONTENTS

PREFACE

These translations were prepared in the summer of 1985. Originally there were going to be a half-dozen or so. Or, more accurately, originally there weren't going to be any at all. I had, at the time, already done a good deal of the work on my panoramic collection, *The Fabulists French: Nine Centuries of the French Verse Fable in Translation,* and had intended, upon first reflection, to exclude from that volume the prototypic and seminal La Fontaine, certainly no stranger to an enlightened readership and not wanting for exposure in the English-speaking world. It seemed to me, in fact, that his absence might be perceived, as they like to say nowadays, as "making a statement" of some arcane kind. (I had even toyed, in admittedly weaker moments, with the notion of affixing a trendy title; something like *Degree Zero of the French Fable: Before and After La Fontaine,* or possibly a more evocative *Fables of the Other...*) But the good sense of longtime friend Evelyn Singer Simha persuaded me to include at least a few La Fontaine examples, even if only for the sake of appearances, not to mention scholarly and aesthetic completeness. Once the spigot was turned on, however, I quickly began to play the sorcerer's apprentice: the work virtually took on a life of its own. The "few" that she had suggested soon outgrew their original purpose and painlessly became the present collection. I am happy to dedicate it to her with affection and gratitude for her interest, her good humor, and above all her unflagging encouragement.

My special thanks to Seamus Heaney for his appreciative reading, as well as to John DuVal, Walter Glanze, Peter O'Malley, and Paul Ruffin for theirs. Likewise to Elizabeth Dulany, Jessica Moseley, and Becky Standard, who know only too well how indispensable has been their patience. Many other friends and associates have been helpfully present at various stages along the way: Lillian Bulwa, Bonnie Edwards, Michael Gibson, Seymour O. Simches, and Caldwell Titcomb. To them all, my gratitude, and to the many others left unnamed. I also want to thank Wesleyan University for its material support; and for their much-valued moral support, Sylvia and Allan Kliman, and, especially, my father. As ever, I take bittersweet pleasure in the memory of my mother, always a source of inspiration, humane and artistic.

The following poems were printed in the *Texas Review* as the 1986 *Texas Review Poetry Award Chapbook:* "The Oak and the Reed," "The Bird

xi

Wounded by an Arrow," "The Lion Brought Down by Man," "The Man with the Wooden Idol," "The Ass with a Load of Holy Relics," "The Stag Who Sees Himself in the Water," "Discord," "The Young Widow," "The Man Who Married a Shrew," "The Acorn and the Pumpkin," "The Old Cat and the Young Mouse," and "Love and Folly."

The following pair appeared in *The Literary Review* (Summer, 1987): "The Man and the Flea" and "The Two Bulls and a Frog."

INTRODUCTION

Often I am asked how a translator translates. And sometimes even why. The "why" is easier to answer than the "how," at least for me. I do it, quite simply, because I enjoy it. No deeper, more transcendent reason than that. For me, artistic translation is a form of recreation; some people play bridge. Perhaps this makes me sound a little hedonistic. Maybe even a little masochistic to boot, given the low esteem in which translators have too often been held in the world of letters. Critics, if they acknowledge them at all, are quick to trumpet their imperfections while seldom troubling to recognize their successes. A translation is like a pane of glass. The better it is, the less it will be noticed. It's only the bubbles and flaws that make it visible, and that consequently attract the observer's attention. Still, those of us who indulge in the craft (or art? or both?) press on despite the odds. Myself, I find it a source of artistic fulfillment, a gauntlet thrown down and a challenge met; even—to wax philosophical—a proof and validation of my creative existence. As I quip to my students (not without some truth in the exaggeration): "Je traduis, donc je suis. . . "

If translation, for some of us, is a form of recreation, it is also, by definition—and for all of us, I hope—a form of re-creation. Which brings us back from the "why" of it to the "how." Obviously there are two basic elements in any translation: the meaning and the manner. Or, to put it in the words of the poet Seamus Heaney, the "tune" and the "tone." I say "obviously," though I realize only too well that there are those among the public who, accustomed to movie subtitles, simultaneous UN interpretations, and such, assume that a translation can be turned out almost automatically, as long as you know what the words mean; fed into one mental slot and cranked out another. That might do for the "tune," at least in everyday, run-of-the-mill discourse. But the "tone" is quite something else again. Especially in what we term "artistic translation." It is made up of all the vague, ill-defined, and yet essential stylistic quirks and nuances, feelings and suggestions, resonances and harmonies— what I like to call the "meta-stuff"—that clothe each author's naked meaning in his own very personal and particular manner.

How does the translator bring across (or "translate," literally) such all-too-vaporous elements? Heaven only knows. Some, alas, don't even bother to try. For them it's only the tune that matters; like those good old interlinear "trots" or "poneys" that got—and may still be getting—

many a student over the pitfalls of Latin. But for those of us who take the job seriously, the tone is no less a part of the original, and somehow it must be rendered if we are going to re-create it. We may not always succeed, but at least we know enough to make the attempt. As for how it's done, while the tune can be taught and learned, the tone, I suspect, is a matter of intuition. No tin ears need apply. It helps though, I'm sure, to like the author in question. And I do mean "like," not merely "admire." That being the case, my present undertaking was much easier than it might appear. A labor of love. There are few French poets as generally well liked as Jean de La Fontaine.

Few, too, whose names are so virtually synonymous with their genres. Say "La Fontaine" to practically any Frenchman, even of modest schooling, and his reply will be "Les Fables..."[1] In fact, with the exception of Aesop—who may well have been more legend than human—no other fabulist of the Western world enjoys such prestige and universal recognition. And rightly so. La Fontaine was, in a manner of speaking, the Beethoven of the verse fable. In France, to be sure, the form had existed before him; but, like the symphony after Beethoven, it would never be the same once he had touched it with his genius. La Fontaine may or may not have known well his French predecessors and their work—the rather traditional, often less-than-inspired fables of the Middle Ages and sixteenth century. There is no question, however, how well his successors knew him and his.[2] His influence is as obvious as it was pervasive and enduring: in form, content, and—individual talent permitting—in style.

As for the form, one need only look at examples. Their very appearance on the printed page tells the tale. After La Fontaine, the vehicle of choice for the verse fable, far and away, will be those irregular, seemingly somewhat capricious *vers libres* of his; the "free verse" that he wrought to perfection and that informs the fabric of most of his *Fables*. (Perhaps "freed verse" would be a more appropriate term, since, unlike the nineteenth- and twentieth-century *vers libres,* La Fontaine's lines, while unshackled from a rigid regularity, remain nonetheless bound by certain conventions of rhyme and meter.)[3] This flexible form, with its profusion of run-on lines, internal rhyming, and natural speech rhythms, afforded La Fontaine the perfect compromise between the poet's innate need for verse and the storyteller's need for the naturalness of prose. The resulting tension between freedom and constraint is one of the greatest charms of his work. The form would be copied with varying degrees of success by generations of followers, from seventeenth-century contemporaries like Furetière and Boursault to twentieth-century descendants like Franc-Nohain and Anouilh, not to mention the scores of eighteenth- and nineteenth-century fabulists: Florian, Dorat, Jauffret, Arnault... The list is long.[4] And most would hew as closely as their individual abilities permitted to the now almost sacrosanct La Fontaine form.

In subject matter too his influence dominates. Some, begging the reader's indulgence for their temerity in treading the same artistic ground as he, will imitate him directly, though with differences dictated by their time, place, and culture. We find him, for example, in a variety of exotic transformations, like Antillean Creole and provincial *patois*. And especially in the work of the legion of neo-Provençal poets—precursors and colleagues of Nobel laureate Frédéric Mistral—who would discover in the verse fable a favorite genre; one that, by its popular appeal, and by La Fontaine's prestige across a wide social spectrum from peasant to intellectual, was seen as a natural art form in which to display the accomplishments of the cultural renaissance. Others would use his work as "pre-text": a literary springboard for a straightforward, primitive kind of "intertextuality" (with none of the tortuous subtleties to which that modern term can give rise). One thinks, for example, of Jean Anouilh's rendition of the famous confrontation between the oak tree and the reed, or of some of Louis Jauffret's fables, which present us with sequels to La Fontaine rather than mere copies: the lamb's posthumous revenge on the arrogant wolf, for instance; or the anorectic fear felt by the sister of the overambitious (and exploding) frog.[5] Still others, like Furetière, take pride in treating subjects left untouched by the master; while some will protest, often a little too demurely, that they dare not treat his subjects, but must content themselves with gleaning whatever "chaff" he has left unpicked. In other words, even when physically absent from their works, La Fontaine continues to make his presence felt. He remains the point of reference for all fabulists that follow. Those who would ignore him merely acknowledge his presence the more they affirm his absence.

Stylistically, of course, none matches his talent, though many have considerable gifts of their own. However they try, none succeeds in infusing his work with the same brand of easygoing La Fontainesque intimacy, the same gently pervasive presence, always at the reader's elbow, ready to inject himself directly with an opinion, an apt comparison, a revealing digression; or indirectly as omniscient observer, privy to the thoughts and sentiments of his characters. "Il ne compose point," says an admiring Jauffret, "il converse."[6] La Fontaine, the reader's constant companion, and, even more, collaborator. . .

It's one of the great ironies of French literary history, understandable nonetheless, that this creative imitator of Aesop *et al.,* who turned simplicity into sophisticated art, should owe so much of his reputation throughout France and the Western world to children, weaned, literally for generations, on his *Fables.* And this, over the objections of a rather humorless Jean-Jacques Rousseau, who impugned La Fontaine's work for a misperceived immorality. Many have pointed out—and here Rousseau was right—that, while perhaps originally intended for the young,[7] most of La Fontaine goes well beyond even a precocious child's comprehension: his portrayal of social types and personification (or "animalization") of human frailties; his philosophical and sometimes religious observations; his frequent allusions, classical and contemporary; his striking yet simple metaphors; his subtle shifts between sarcasm and sincerity. Above all, the need to have lived and experienced the Good and Bad in life, in their many manifestations. This is especially true as La Fontaine moves from the relative simplicity of Books I to VI (1668)—mainly adaptations of the Aesopic corpus—through the progressively weightier and more intellectual fables of Books VII to XI (1678–79) and XII (1694). If a child can grasp the story line of such popular early fables as "The Cricket and the Ant" and "The Crow and the Fox," the full meaning of such later ones as "The Value of Knowledge" and "Love and Folly," to name but two, will surely be lost on him. And so too the myriad subtleties of style that make La Fontaine, indeed, La Fontaine. Beyond any child's artistic appreciation are the flow of lines, sweeping along their unobtrusive rhymes and rhythms in a show of seemingly effortless craftsmanship; the dramatic tone, the visual imagery, the intimacy, the wit. . . All much too sophisticated, even in the early and best-known fables, for any child's aesthetic. And for the tin-eared, tin-souled adult as well, if such there be, who fails to appreciate this master of his genre, this standard by which all the rest are measured.

One might ask why, if I admire (and like) La Fontaine so much, I stopped after translating only fifty of his *Fables,* about one-fifth, albeit a sampling from all the twelve books. Let me assure my friends that it's not just to have an alliterative title: *Fifty Fables of La Fontaine.* Perhaps it's because I prefer to take my pleasure in measured doses, and to leave some joy for the future; the joy of more re-creation (and recreation) with that posthumous but ever-present collaborator whom the French call simply "notre bon La Fontaine," and, even more affectionately, "le bonhomme Jean."[8]

NOTES

1. The same Frenchman would probably be hard put to name any other practitioner of the form, although the verse fable—one of the most vigorous, if least known, of the French poetic genres—has been practiced from the Middle Ages uninterruptedly to modern times. (For a comprehensive view, see my volume, *The Fabulists French: Nine Centuries of the French Verse Fable in Translation* [Urbana: University of Illinois Press, forthcoming].)

2. In the preface to his first collection (1668), La Fontaine calls attention, albeit modestly, to his role as initiator, envisioning the possibility that his work "fera naître à

d'autres personnes l'envie de porter la chose plus loin." As for his own predecessors, he readily acknowledges his debt to Aesopic models, at some length in that preface and more pithily in his dedicatory verses to the Dauphin: "Je chante les héros dont Ésope est le père..." It is generally agreed however that, while he seems to have been familiar with some of the French (and even Italian) fabulists of the sixteenth century—the "modernes" to whom he refers—he probably knew little if anything of his medieval French antecedents. (For examples of their work, see *The Fabulists French,* as well as my earlier collection *Fables from Old French: Aesop's Beasts and Bumpkins* [Middletown, Conn.: Wesleyan University Press, 1982].)

3. Even the term "freed verse" might lead to confusion, since it is used to translate the *vers libérés* of nineteenth-century Symbolists like Verlaine. The form espoused by La Fontaine—and occasionally used as well by contemporaries like Corneille and Molière—is in fact closer, at least in spirit, to the restrained freedom of those *vers libérés* than to the total freedom of the subsequent *vers libres.*

4. Too long, indeed, for inclusion here. Several dozen are translated and discussed in *The Fabulists French;* among them, a number of the adapters into Creole, *patois,* and neo-Provençal, referred to below, as well as the "sequel"-writers Anouilh and Jauffret, among others.

5. See "The Oak and the Reed" (p. 19), "The Wolf and the Lamb" (p. 13), and "The Frog Who Would Grow as Big as the Ox" (p. 7). Anouilh's "sequel" is found in his collection of *Fables* (Paris: La Table Ronde, 1962), pp. 21–22; Jauffret's in his *Fables nouvelles,* 2d ed., 2 vols. (Paris: Béchet, 1826), II:164, 284–85.

6. Jauffret, I:xiii. In a fanciful preface to his collection, entitled "L'Élysée des fabulistes," Jauffret puts the words into the mouth of the eighteenth-century fabulist Florian, discussing with his colleagues in the Great Beyond the luminaries of the genre.

7. At least so we are led to believe by his remarks to the six-year-old Dauphin, in the opening paragraph of his letter of dedication: "C'est un entretien convenable à vos premières années. Vous êtes en un âge où l'amusement et les jeux sont permis aux princes; mais en même temps vous devez donner quelques-unes de vos pensées à des réflexions sérieuses. Tout cela se rencontre aux fables que nous devons à Ésope. L'apparence en est puérile, je le confesse; mais ces puérilités servent d'enveloppe à des vérités importantes."

8. The single most useful work in the La Fontaine bibliography remains the venerable eleven-volume critical edition of Henri Regnier, *Œuvres de J. de la Fontaine,* rev. ed. (Paris: Hachette, 1883–92), in the series "Les Grands Écrivains de la France." It is a mine of pertinent details, not only as regards the provenance of the *Fables,* but also for its thorough explanation of allusions and references, as well as its biography of the poet, a grammatical study of his style, and an extensive and systematic lexicon. (It is the text of that edition that I reproduce, straying from it only occasionally, to correct insignificant misprints.) I shall resist the temptation of appending to these brief remarks a listing of the vast bibliographical information on La Fontaine in French. Specialists don't need it, other scholars know where to find it, and laymen wouldn't use it. For the general reader, however, uncomfortable with French but interested in the poet's life, times, and art, the following works are available in English:

Jean Dominique Biard, *The Style of La Fontaine's "Fables"* (Oxford: Blackwell, 1966)
Richard Danner, *Patterns of Irony in the "Fables" of La Fontaine* (Athens: Ohio University
  Press, 1985)

Margaret Guiton, *La Fontaine, Poet and Counterpoet* (New Brunswick, N.J.: Rutgers University Press, 1961)

Frank Hamel, *Jean de La Fontaine* (London: Stanley Paul, 1911; rpt. Port Washington, N.Y.: Kennikat Press, 1970)

Ethel M. King, *Jean de La Fontaine* (Brooklyn: Gaus, 1970)

Agnes Ethel Mackey, *La Fontaine and His Friends* (New York: Braziller, 1973)

Monica Sutherland, *La Fontaine* (London: Jonathan Cape, 1953; rpt. 1974)

Marie-Odile Sweetser, *La Fontaine* (Boston: Twayne, 1987)

Philip Wadsworth, *Young La Fontaine* (Evanston: Northwestern University Press, 1952)

The following, while devoted primarily to La Fontaine's less generally admired *Contes* (1665–74), contains stylistic observations applicable as well to his *Fables:*

John Clarke Lapp, *The Esthetics of Negligence: La Fontaine's "Contes"* (Cambridge: Cambridge University Press, 1971)

Fifty Fables of La Fontaine

LA CIGALE ET LA FOURMI

La Cigale, ayant chanté
Tout l'été,
Se trouva fort dépourvue
Quand la bise fut venue :
Pas un seul petit morceau
De mouche ou de vermisseau.
Elle alla crier famine
Chez la Fourmi sa voisine,
La priant de lui prêter
Quelque grain pour subsister
Jusqu'à la saison nouvelle.
« Je vous paierai, lui dit-elle,
Avant l'oût, foi d'animal,
Intérêt et principal. »
La Fourmi n'est pas prêteuse :
C'est là son moindre défaut.
« Que faisiez-vous au temps chaud?
Dit-elle à cette emprunteuse.
— Nuit et jour à tout venant
Je chantois, ne vous déplaise.
— Vous chantiez? j'en suis fort aise :
Eh bien! dansez maintenant. »

THE CRICKET AND THE ANT

The cricket, having sung her song
           All summer long,
Found—when the winter winds blew free—
Her cupboard bare as bare could be;
Nothing to greet her hungering eye:
No merest crumb of worm or fly.
She went next door to cry her plight
To neighbor ant, hoping she might
Take pity on her, and befriend her,
Eke out a bit of grain to lend her,
And see her through till spring: "What say you?
On insect's honor, I'll repay you
Well before fall. With interest, too!"
Our ant—no willing lender she!
Least of her faults!—replied: "I see!
Tell me, my friend, what did you do
While it was warm?" "Well. . . Night and day,
I sang my song for all to hear."
"You sang, you say? How nice, my dear!
Now go and dance your life away!"

(I, 1)

The Crow and the Fox

LE CORBEAU ET LE RENARD

Maître Corbeau, sur un arbre perché,
Tenoit en son bec un fromage.
Maître Renard, par l'odeur alléché,
Lui tint à peu près ce langage :
« Hé! bonjour, Monsieur du Corbeau.
Que vous êtes joli! que vous me semblez beau!
Sans mentir, si votre ramage
Se rapporte à votre plumage,
Vous êtes le phénix des hôtes de ces bois. »
A ces mots le Corbeau ne se sent pas de joie;
Et pour montrer sa belle voix,
Il ouvre un large bec, laisse tomber sa proie.
Le Renard s'en saisit, et dit : « Mon bon Monsieur,
Apprenez que tout flatteur
Vit aux dépens de celui qui l'écoute :
Cette leçon vaut bien un fromage, sans doute. »
Le Corbeau, honteux et confus,
Jura, mais un peu tard, qu'on ne l'y prendroit plus.

THE CROW AND THE FOX

Perched on a treetop, Master Crow
Was clutching in his bill a cheese,
When Master Fox, sniffing the fragrant breeze,
Came by and, more or less, addressed him so:
"Good day to you, Your Ravenhood!
How beautiful you are! How fine! How fair!
Ah! Truly, if your song could but compare
To all the rest, I'm sure you should
Be dubbed the *rara avis* of the wood!"
The crow, beside himself with joy and pride,
Begins to caw. He opens wide
His gawking beak; lets go the cheese; it
Falls to the ground. The fox is there to seize it,
Saying: "You see? Be edified:
Flatterers thrive on fools' credulity.
The lesson's worth a cheese, don't you agree?"
The crow, shamefaced and flustered, swore—
Too late, however: "Nevermore!"

(I, 2)

The Frog Who Would Grow as Big as the Ox

LA GRENOUILLE QUI SE VEUT FAIRE
AUSSI GROSSE QUE LE BŒUF

Une Grenouille vit un Bœuf
Qui lui sembla de belle taille.
Elle, qui n'étoit pas grosse en tout comme un œuf,
Envieuse, s'étend, et s'enfle, et se travaille,
Pour égaler l'animal en grosseur,
Disant : « Regardez bien, ma sœur;
Est-ce assez? dites-moi; n'y suis-je point encore?
— Nenni. — M'y voici donc? — Point du tout. — M'y voilà?
— Vous n'en approchez point. » La chétive pécore
S'enfla si bien qu'elle creva.

Le monde est plein de gens qui ne sont pas plus sages :
Tout bourgeois veut bâtir comme les grands seigneurs,
Tout petit prince a des ambassadeurs,
Tout marquis veut avoir des pages.[1]

THE FROG WHO WOULD GROW
AS BIG AS THE OX

A frog espies an ox
Of elegant dimension.
Herself no bigger than an egg, she gapes and gawks
In envy at his grandeur. Her intention?
To grow as huge as he. And so,
Huffing and puffing, all a-fuss, a-fret,
She asks: "Look, sister, have I done it?" "No!"
"And now?" "Nay, nay!" "There! Have I yet?"
"Not even close!" The paltry mite—galled, goaded—
Swelled up so well that she exploded.

This world of ours is full of foolish creatures too:
Commoners want to build chateaus;
Each princeling wants his royal retinue;
Each count, his squires. And so it goes.

(I, 3)

7

LES DEUX MULETS

Deux Mulets cheminoient, l'un d'avoine chargé,
    L'autre portant l'argent de la gabelle.
Celui-ci, glorieux d'une charge si belle,
N'eût voulu pour beaucoup en être soulagé.
        Il marchoit d'un pas relevé,
        Et faisoit sonner sa sonnette :
        Quand l'ennemi se présentant,
        Comme il en vouloit à l'argent,
Sur le Mulet du fisc une troupe se jette,
        Le saisit au frein et l'arrête.
        Le Mulet, en se défendant,
Se sent percer de coups; il gémit, il soupire.
« Est-ce donc là, dit-il, ce qu'on m'avoit promis?
Ce Mulet qui me suit du danger se retire;
        Et moi j'y tombe, et je péris!
        — Ami, lui dit son camarade,
Il n'est pas toujours bon d'avoir un haut emploi :
Si tu n'avois servi qu'un meunier, comme moi,
        Tu ne serois pas si malade. »

THE TWO MULES

Two mules there were, each with his heavy pack,
Wending their way. One carried on his back
    A load of oats and nothing more.
    The other, belled and bridled, bore
A sack of money for the tax-collector.
    Proud of his noble charge, he swore
    Ever to be its staunch protector.
That is, until some miscreants happened on him,
Robbed him, and rained blow after blow upon him.
    Then, all at once grown circumspecter:
    "Ah me," he sighed, "nobody said
That with my gold I well might end up dead!
    Somebody should have told me so!
That mule behind lopes footloose, fancy-free,
And leaves me to my torment and my woe."
The latter smiled: "My friend of high degree,
    Best not to work for men of wealth.
Had you served but a miller, just like me,
I daresay you would be in better health!"

(I, 4)

LE RAT DE VILLE ET
LE RAT DES CHAMPS

Autrefois le Rat de ville
Invita le Rat des champs,
D'une façon fort civile,
A des reliefs d'ortolans.

Sur un tapis de Turquie
Le couvert se trouva mis.
Je laisse à penser la vie
Que firent ces deux amis.

Le régal fut fort honnête :
Rien ne manquoit au festin;
Mais quelqu'un troubla la fête
Pendant qu'ils étoient en train.

A la porte de la salle
Ils entendirent du bruit :
Le Rat de ville détale;
Son camarade le suit.

Le bruit cesse, on se retire :
Rats en campagne aussitôt;
Et le citadin de dire :
« Achevons tout notre rôt.

— C'est assez, dit le rustique;
Demain vous viendrez chez moi.
Ce n'est pas que je me pique
De tous vos festins de roi;

Mais rien ne vient m'interrompre :
Je mange tout à loisir.
Adieu donc. Fi du plaisir
Que la crainte peut corrompre! »

THE CITY RAT AND
THE COUNTRY RAT

A certain rat—a city type—
    Once asked a country rat
To come and dine on scraps of snipe,
    Quite civilly at that.

Upon a rug of Turkish weave,
    Outspread, lay the collation.
Just how the pair behaved, I leave
    To your imagination.

The meal was all two rats could wish;
    But as they took their leisure,
Something—most likely humanish—
    Came by to spoil their pleasure.

Outside the door where they were eating:
    Noises of frightful kind!
Off flees the city rat, retreating;
    Country friend close behind.

Next moment, silence. Rats come back
    Once Danger has departed.
Says city dweller: "Let's attack
    That tasty feast we started!"

Says rustic: "No, friend millionaire.
    Tomorrow you come visit.
It's not that I can match your fare—
    It's just not safe here, is it?

"I'm for much simpler meals, no question!
    Bye-bye. I'd rather be
Able to eat unworriedly—
    And free of indigestion!"

(I, 9)

The Wolf and the Lamb

LE LOUP ET L'AGNEAU

La raison du plus fort est toujours la meilleure :
Nous l'allons montrer tout à l'heure.

Un Agneau se désaltéroit
Dans le courant d'une onde pure.
Un Loup survient à jeun, qui cherchoit aventure,
Et que la faim en ces lieux attiroit.
« Qui te rend si hardi de troubler mon breuvage?
Dit cet animal plein de rage :
Tu seras châtié de ta témérité.
— Sire, répond l'Agneau, que Votre Majesté
Ne se mette pas en colère;
Mais plutôt qu'elle considère
Que je me vas désaltérant
Dans le courant,
Plus de vingt pas au-dessous d'Elle;
Et que par conséquent, en aucune façon,
Je ne puis troubler sa boisson.
— Tu la troubles, reprit cette bête cruelle;
Et je sais que de moi tu médis l'an passé.
— Comment l'aurois-je fait si je n'étois pas né?
Reprit l'Agneau; je tette encor ma mère.
— Si ce n'est toi, c'est donc ton frère.
— Je n'en ai point. — C'est donc quelqu'un des tiens;
Car vous ne m'épargnez guère,
Vous, vos bergers, et vos chiens.
On me l'a dit : il faut que je me venge. »
Là-dessus, au fond des forêts
Le Loup l'emporte, et puis le mange,
Sans autre forme de procès.

THE WOLF AND THE LAMB

The strongest argue best, and always win.
Read on: you'll find the proof thereof herein.

    A certain lamb his thirst was slaking
    Next to a crystal stream, when lo!,
A hungry wolf drew near, his leisure taking,
Hoping to find a tasty meal or so.
    The beast in fearsome tones snarled, snorted:
"How dare you foul my drink! I'll make you pay!"
"Pardon me, Sire," meekly the lamb retorted,
    "But if Your Majesty, I pray—
        With due respect—
    Would please consider, in effect,
The facts, I'm sure that he would plainly see
I'm twenty paces farther down than he.
    I fail to fathom what he's thinking,
Since in no way can I disturb his drinking."
    "Yes, yes! You do! . . . And that's not all!"
Replied the wolf. "I'll thank you to recall,
    Last year you cursed me!" "Me? But how?
I wasn't even born, Sire! Ask my mother!
I'm still a suckling." "Then it was your brother!"
"Brother? I haven't any." "Then, I vow,
It was some other of your scheming kin.
You're all the same, plotting to do me in—
    Sheep, shepherds, hounds! Well, tit for tat!"
    Wherewith the beast, in all his fury,
    Whisked him into the woods; whereat
He wolfed him down. And that was that—
        No judge, no jury.

                    (I, 10)

LES VOLEURS ET L'ÂNE

Pour un Âne enlevé deux Voleurs se battoient :
L'un vouloit le garder, l'autre le vouloit vendre.
    Tandis que coups de poing trottoient,
Et que nos champions songeoient à se défendre,
    Arrive un troisième larron
    Qui saisit maître Aliboron.[1]

L'Âne, c'est quelquefois une pauvre province :
    Les voleurs sont tel ou tel prince,
Comme le Transylvain, le Turc, et le Hongrois.
    Au lieu de deux, j'en ai rencontré trois :
    Il est assez de cette marchandise.
De nul d'eux n'est souvent la province conquise :
Un quart voleur survient, qui les accorde net
    En se saisissant du Baudet.

THE THIEVES AND THE ASS

They tell about two thieves who fought
Over a stolen ass: one thought
It ought be kept; the other, sold. Fists flew,
Blows fell. And while our heroes sought
To prove their point with derring-do,
Another brigand came upon
The scene, and seized Master Aliboron.

So too with military handiwork.
Some petty province is the prize;
And while the warring princes agonize—
Hungarian, Transylvanian, Turk
(Not just a thieving two, but three: there is
No limit to such merchandise!),
A fourth steps in; resolves the fight: the ass is his!

(I, 13)

LE COQ ET LA PERLE

Un jour un Coq détourna
Une Perle, qu'il donna
Au beau premier lapidaire.
« Je la crois fine, dit-il;
Mais le moindre grain de mil
Seroit bien mieux mon affaire. »

Un ignorant hérita
D'un manuscrit, qu'il porta
Chez son voisin le libraire.
« Je crois, dit-il, qu'il est bon;
Mais le moindre ducaton
Seroit bien mieux mon affaire. »[1]

THE COCK AND THE PEARL

A cock turned up a pearl, and went
Straight to the jeweller. "Yes, I should
Be pleased," he cackled, discontent.
"But it's a fact: unhappily,
A simple grain of millet would
Be of much greater good to me."

A fool inherited a book—
A fine old manuscript—and stood
Complaining to a bookman: "Look,
It's precious. . . Yes, I quite agree.
But just the merest ducat could
Be of much greater good to me."

(I, 20)

LE CHÊNE ET LE ROSEAU

Le Chêne un jour dit au Roseau :
« Vous avez bien sujet d'accuser la nature;
Un roitelet pour vous est un pesant fardeau;
Le moindre vent, qui d'aventure
Fait rider la face de l'eau,
Vous oblige à baisser la tête,
Cependant que mon front, au Caucase pareil,
Non content d'arrêter les rayons du soleil,
Brave l'effort de la tempête.
Tout vous est aquilon, tout me semble zéphyr.
Encor si vous naissiez à l'abri du feuillage
Dont je couvre le voisinage,
Vous n'auriez pas tant à souffrir :
Je vous défendrois de l'orage;
Mais vous naissez le plus souvent
Sur les humides bords des royaumes du vent.
La nature envers vous me semble bien injuste.
— Votre compassion, lui répondit l'arbuste,
Part d'un bon naturel; mais quittez ce souci :
Les vents me sont moins qu'à vous redoutables;
Je plie, et ne romps pas. Vous avez jusqu'ici
Contre leurs coups épouvantables
Résisté sans courber le dos;
Mais attendons la fin. » Comme il disoit ces mots,
Du bout de l'horizon accourt avec furie
Le plus terrible des enfants
Que le Nord eût portés jusque-là dans ses flancs.
L'arbre tient bon; le Roseau plie.
Le vent redouble ses efforts,
Et fait si bien qu'il déracine
Celui de qui la tête au ciel étoit voisine,
Et dont les pieds touchoient à l'empire des morts.

THE OAK AND THE REED

The oak one day spoke to the reed: "I swear,
You have good cause to fret at Nature. Why,
Even a wren weighs more than you can bear.
And when the slightest breeze that, by the by,
Ripples the water's face, down must you bow;
    Whereas my broad and mighty brow,
Caucasus-like against the sun and sky,
    Defies the storm. For you, see how
Each gust is like a northwind blast; for me,
Mere zephyr. Now, had you the luck to be
Born in my shadow, nothing need affect you,
    Safe from the wind's tempestuous whim,
Beneath my overspreading leaf and limb.
For I, the mighty oak, I would protect you!
But no! Denied by Nature's harsh neglect, you
Grow by the dank dominions of the wind.
    Poor wretch!" "Monsieur," replied the reed,
"It's kind of you to be so sore chagrined
On my account. I thank you. But, no need!
I fear the winds far less than you, my friend.
You see, I never break; I only bend.
    Till now, indeed, you have withstood
Their frightful force unbowed. So far so good.
    But wait. We haven't seen the end."
    As thus he spoke, from out beyond
The far horizon, like the crack of doom,
There looms the fiercest offspring ever spawned
    From deep within the Northwind's womb.
Oak holds. . . Reed bends. . . Wind blows. . . Then more and more,
Till it uproots the one who, just before,
Had risen heavenward with lofty head,
Whose feet had reached the empire of the dead.

(I, 22)

The Two Bulls and a Frog

Deux Taureaux combattoient à qui posséderoit
Une Génisse avec l'empire.
Une Grenouille en soupiroit.
« Qu'avez-vous? » se mit à lui dire
Quelqu'un du peuple croassant.
« Et ne voyez-vous pas, dit-elle,
Que la fin de cette querelle
Sera l'exil de l'un; que l'autre, le chassant,
Le fera renoncer aux campagnes fleuries?
Il ne régnera plus sur l'herbe des prairies,
Viendra dans nos marais régner sur les roseaux;
Et nous foulant aux pieds jusques au fond des eaux,
Tantôt l'une, et puis l'autre, il faudra qu'on pâtisse
Du combat qu'a causé Madame la Génisse. »
Cette crainte étoit de bon sens.
L'un des Taureaux en leur demeure
S'alla cacher à leurs dépens :
Il en écrasoit vingt par heure.

Hélas! on voit que de tout temps
Les petits ont pâti des sottises des grands.

THE TWO BULLS AND A FROG

A pair of amorous bulls stood vying
Over a heifer both would woo and service.
"Misery me!" a frog sat sighing,
Eyeing their combat—timorous, nervous;
Whereat one of her croaking kin
Queried: "Good gracious, why the fuss?"
"Why?" cried the frog. "For us, that's why! For us!
One of those two is sure to win;
And when he drives his rival out,
Far from their green and flowering fields, what then? . . .
Then he'll come stomping over swamp and fen,
Trampling our reeds! And us as well, no doubt!
Tomorrow we'll be dead. And why? Because here, now,
Two bulls are fighting for some silly cow!"
Frog's dread predictions come to pass.
When bull, defeated, seeks their dank morass,
Twenty compatriots an hour croak
Their final croak: a crushing fate!

Alas, 'twas ever thus. The little folk
Have always paid for follies of the great.

(II, 4)

The Bird Wounded by an Arrow

L'OISEAU BLESSÉ D'UNE FLÈCHE

Mortellement atteint d'une flèche empennée,
Un Oiseau déploroit sa triste destinée,
Et disoit, en souffrant un surcroît de douleur :
« Faut-il contribuer à son propre malheur!
    Cruels humains! vous tirez de nos ailes
De quoi faire voler ces machines mortelles.
Mais ne vous moquez point, engeance sans pitié :
Souvent il vous arrive un sort comme le nôtre.
Des enfants de Japet toujours une moitié
    Fournira des armes à l'autre. »

THE BIRD WOUNDED BY AN ARROW

Mortally wounded by a feathered dart,
A bird laments his pain, pours out his heart,
Tortured the more with guilt for his condition:
    "Barbarous Man! You pluck our wings
To rend the air with those infernal things
And make us authors of our own perdition!
    Well, don't be quick to mock and chide.
Cruel race, you really have no right to laugh:
One half of Japhet's progeny provide
    The weapons for the other half."

(II, 6)

The Lion and the Gnat

LE LION ET LE MOUCHERON

« Va-t’en, chétif insecte, excrément de la terre! »
　　　C’est en ces mots que le Lion
　　　Parloit un jour au Moucheron.
　　　L’autre lui déclara la guerre.
« Penses-tu, lui dit-il, que ton titre de roi
　　　Me fasse peur ni me soucie?
　　　Un bœuf est plus puissant que toi :
　　　Je le mène à ma fantaisie. »
　　　A peine il achevoit ces mots
　　　Que lui-même il sonna la charge,
　　　Fut le trompette et le héros.
　　　Dans l’abord il se met au large;
　　　Puis prend son temps, fond sur le cou
　　　Du Lion, qu’il rend presque fou.
Le quadrupède écume, et son œil étincelle;
Il rugit; on se cache, on tremble à l’environ;
　　　Et cette alarme universelle
　　　Est l’ouvrage d’un moucheron.
Un avorton de mouche en cent lieux le harcelle:
Tantôt pique l’échine, et tantôt le museau,
　　　Tantôt entre au fond du naseau.
La rage alors se trouve à son faîte montée,
L’invisible ennemi triomphe, et rit de voir
Qu’il n’est griffe ni dent en la bête irritée
Qui de la mettre en sang ne fasse son devoir.
Le malheureux Lion se déchire lui-même,
Fait résonner sa queue à l’entour de ses flancs,
Bat l’air, qui n’en peut mais; et sa fureur extrême
Le fatigue, l’abat : le voilà sur les dents.
L’insecte du combat se retire avec gloire :
Comme il sonna la charge, il sonne la victoire,
Va partout l’annoncer, et rencontre en chemin
　　　L’embuscade d’une araignée;
　　　Il y rencontre aussi sa fin.

Quelle chose par là nous peut être enseignée?
J’en vois deux, dont l’une est qu’entre nos ennemis
Les plus à craindre sont souvent les plus petits;
L’autre, qu’aux grands périls tel a pu se soustraire,
　　　Qui périt pour la moindre affaire.

THE LION AND THE GNAT

"Be gone, vile bug! Scum of the earth, away!"
    So cried the lion to the gnat;
    Whereat the latter warned him: "That
    Means war! You think that sobriquet
Of yours, that title, frightens me? You, 'king'?
    The bull is mightier than you;
    And yet, my friend, I make him do
    My bidding, at the slightest sting!"
    His brazen words still echoing,
The hero—trumpeter and cavalier
    In one—goes falling to the rear,
    Pauses, then sounds the charge, and does
    What gnats do best. That is, abuzz,
    He makes straight for the lion's neck.
The king fumes, froths, and, rearing for the fight,
Glares, roars, sets all the forest folk affright,
Cowering in their lairs. And why? Because a speck—
    The puniest of flies, a mite,
    A midge—nettles him here, there, everywhere.
At length the brash attacker makes his way
    Right up the lion's nose. Despair!
In agony and utter disarray
    He lashes out in rage. . . Bites, claws. . .
In vain: invisible, the enemy
    Reveling in his mastery,
Laughs at the lion's efforts—nay, guffaws
    To see him flail his deadly paws
And flashing tail against his bleeding flanks,
Until, at last, he lies done in, undone.
    Victorious, the gnat gives thanks,
Trumpets his triumph, gloriously won,
All round about the woods. But as he goes,
He meets a spider's web—O woe of woes!—
    And in a trice his fate is sealed.

    Now, what's the moral here revealed?
In fact, I see a double lesson. First:
Our smallest enemies can be the worst;
Second: we may escape a great oppressor
    Only to fall before a lesser.

(II, 9)

The Cock and the Fox

LE COQ ET LE RENARD

Sur la branche d'un arbre étoit en sentinelle
  Un vieux Coq adroit et matois.
« Frère, dit un Renard, adoucissant sa voix,
  Nous ne sommes plus en querelle:
  Paix générale cette fois.
Je viens te l'annoncer; descends, que je t'embrasse.
  Ne me retarde point, de grâce;
Je dois faire aujourd'hui vingt postes sans manquer.
  Les tiens et toi pouvez vaquer,
  Sans nulle crainte, à vos affaires;
  Nous vous y servirons en frères.
  Faites-en les feux dès ce soir,
  Et cependant viens recevoir
  Le baiser d'amour fraternelle.
— Ami, reprit le Coq, je ne pouvois jamais
Apprendre une plus douce et meilleure nouvelle
  Que celle
  De cette paix;
  Et ce m'est une double joie
De la tenir de toi. Je vois deux Lévriers,
  Qui, je m'assure, sont courriers
  Que pour ce sujet on envoie :
Ils vont vite, et seront dans un moment à nous.
Je descends : nous pourrons nous entre-baiser tous.
— Adieu, dit le Renard, ma traite est longue à faire :
Nous nous réjouirons du succès de l'affaire
  Une autre fois. » Le galand aussitôt
  Tire ses grègues, gagne au haut,
  Mal content de son stratagème.
  Et notre vieux Coq en soi-même
  Se mit à rire de sa peur;
Car c'est double plaisir de tromper le trompeur.

THE COCK AND THE FOX

A cock, on guard, was perching in a tree—
    One of your elder, wilier cocks.
"Brother," in dulcet tones warbled a fox,
    "Peace unto you, your family,
And all your kind! That's what I've come to say.
    Fly down. Let me embrace you. Quick!
I've got some twenty stops to make today,
In every corner of your bailiwick,
    To spread the news: now you and yours
    Are free to go about your chores
    Without the slightest trepidation.
What's more, I'll even help! Tonight, the celebration:
    Bonfires and all! But for the nonce,
Come, brother, let me kiss you." And the cock's response:
    "My friend, your welcome declaration
    Fills me with cheer. And it behooves me
    To say how much
    It moves me.
    Double the joy, indeed, when such
Fair tidings come from you yourself. No doubt
    That pair of hounds I see, about
To join us, are the couriers sent to bring
Official word of this fair happening.
They're almost here. . . Yes, I'll come down. Then you and I,
    And they, and all of us, can kiss and kiss!"
    "They?" cries the fox. "That is. . . Bye-bye!
    I mustn't miss my calls. We'll try
To find a better time to toast all this!"
    And off he runs in fright, frustrated.
    Laughing, our crafty cock, elated,
Watches his flight. Revenge was never sweeter.
What greater pleasure than to cheat the cheater!

                                       (II, 15)

The Wolf and the Stork

LE LOUP ET LA CICOGNE

Les Loups mangent gloutonnement.
Un Loup donc étant de frairie
Se pressa, dit-on, tellement
Qu'il en pensa perdre la vie :
Un os lui demeura bien avant au gosier.
De bonheur pour ce Loup, qui ne pouvoit crier,
Près de là passe une Cicogne.
Il lui fait signe; elle accourt.
Voilà l'opératrice aussitôt en besogne.
Elle retira l'os; puis, pour un si bon tour,
Elle demanda son salaire.
« Votre salaire? dit le Loup :
Vous riez, ma bonne commère!
Quoi? ce n'est pas encor beaucoup
D'avoir de mon gosier retiré votre cou?
Allez, vous êtes une ingrate :
Ne tombez jamais sous ma patte. »

THE WOLF AND THE STORK

A wolf—a glutton like his brothers:
No worse nor better than the others—
Gulped down a meal so hurriedly
He almost died. What happened was as follows:
One day, he accidentally swallows
Part of a bone. It won't come free.
Trying to shout, he can't get out a sound,
And gestures to a stork who, coming round
Just then (as luck would have it), sets about
To probe his gullet with her beak and pull it out.
"There!" says the bird. "Now then, my pay. . .
Seeing I've saved you, sir, from choking. . . "
"Pay?" jeers the wolf. "You must be joking!
Some gratitude! It's pay enough, I'd say,
That I should let you walk away
And save your neck, my cackling hen!
Now don't you let me catch you here again!"

(III, 9)

LE LION ABATTU PAR L'HOMME

On exposoit une peinture
Où l'artisan avoit tracé
Un lion d'immense stature
Par un seul homme terrassé.
Les regardants en tiroient gloire.
Un Lion en passant rabattit leur caquet.
« Je vois bien, dit-il, qu'en effet
On vous donne ici la victoire;
Mais l'ouvrier vous a déçus :
Il avoit liberté de feindre.
Avec plus de raison nous aurions le dessus,
Si mes confrères savoient peindre. »

THE LION BROUGHT DOWN BY MAN

A canvas at an exposition
Pictures a lion of enormous size
    Felled by one man. With pride-filled eyes
    The public views the fine rendition,
    Until a lion, passing through,
    Gives them a proper talking-to:
    "It's true, you've won this competition,
But only in your artist's fantasy!
    This painted victory is yours;
    But don't be fooled, my friends!" he roars.
    "Imagine what the scene would be
If my confreres could paint as well as he."

(III, 10)

The Fox and the Grapes

LE RENARD ET LES RAISINS

Certain Renard gascon, d'autres disent normand,[1]
Mourant presque de faim, vit au haut d'une treille
    Des Raisins mûrs apparemment,
    Et couverts d'une peau vermeille.
Le galand en eût fait volontiers un repas;
    Mais comme il n'y pouvoit atteindre :
« Ils sont trop verts, dit-il, et bons pour des goujats. »

    Fit-il pas mieux que de se plaindre?

THE FOX AND THE GRAPES

Starving, a fox from Gascony. . . Some say
    He was a Norman. . . Anyway,
He spies a bunch of grapes high on a vine,
    With skin the shade of deep red wine,
    Ripe for the tastiest of dining,
But out of reach, hard though he perseveres.
    "Bah! Fit for boors! Still green!" he sneers.

Wasn't that better than to stand there whining?

                 (III, 11)

LE CYGNE ET LE CUISINIER

Dans une ménagerie
De volatiles remplie
Vivoient le Cygne et l'Oison :
Celui-là destiné pour les regards du maître;
Celui-ci, pour son goût : l'un qui se piquoit d'être
Commensal du jardin; l'autre, de la maison.
Des fossés du château faisant leurs galeries,
Tantôt on les eût vus côte à côte nager,
Tantôt courir sur l'onde, et tantôt se plonger,
Sans pouvoir satisfaire à leurs vaines envies.
Un jour le Cuisinier, ayant trop bu d'un coup,
Prit pour oison le Cygne; et le tenant au cou,
Il alloit l'égorger, puis le mettre en potage.
L'oiseau, prêt à mourir, se plaint en son ramage.
Le Cuisinier fut fort surpris,
Et vit bien qu'il s'étoit mépris.
« Quoi? je mettrois, dit-il, un tel chanteur en soupe!
Non, non, ne plaise aux Dieux que jamais ma main coupe
La gorge à qui s'en sert si bien! »

Ainsi dans les dangers qui nous suivent en croupe
Le doux parler ne nuit de rien.

THE SWAN AND THE COOK

A noble's birdhouse, once upon
A time, housed flocks of every feather,
All in a multitude together.
Among them were a gosling and a swan:
The second, meant to grace His Lordship's gaze;
The first, to feast not eyes but palate on.
The one—one of your fancy popinjays—
Fancied himself more bosom friend than beast;
The other, at the very least,
A household pet. At any rate, our couple went,
Day in, day out, swimming about the moat,
Gliding and bobbing to their hearts' content.
One day the cook—drunken impenitent—
Mistaking swan for goose, was going to slit his throat
And stick him in the stew, when lo!
The bird, about to die, sings out his woe.
Cook beats his breast: "Good God! You nincompoop!
A voice like that! And you were going to throw
That golden gullet in the soup!"

When dangers threaten and life's trials alarm,
A little sweet talk does no harm.

(III, 12)

The Lion Grown Old

LE LION DEVENU VIEUX

Le Lion, terreur des forêts,
Chargé d'ans et pleurant son antique prouesse,
Fut enfin attaqué par ses propres sujets,
Devenus forts par sa foiblesse.
Le Cheval s'approchant lui donne un coup de pied;
Le Loup, un coup de dent; le Bœuf, un coup de corne.
Le malheureux Lion, languissant, triste, et morne,
Peut à peine rugir, par l'âge estropié.
Il attend son destin, sans faire aucunes plaintes;
Quand voyant l'Âne même à son antre accourir :
« Ah! c'est trop, lui dit-il; je voulois bien mourir;
Mais c'est mourir deux fois que souffrir tes atteintes. »

THE LION GROWN OLD

The lion, terror of the forest, lies
Laden with years, lamenting feats of prowess past.
His loyal subjects, grown at last
More daring at his imminent demise,
Come and attack him with their newfound strength,
Each in his own most brutish wise:
Horse kicks, wolf bites, ox butts and gores... At length,
Resigned—crippled, too weak to roar—he spies
The ass approaching! O disgrace unbounded!
"I don't mind facing death," he sighs,
Eyeing the ass. "But you!" he cries.
"To suffer your abuse is death compounded!"

(III, 14)

The Ape and the Dolphin

LE SINGE ET LE DAUPHIN

C'étoit chez les Grecs un usage
Que sur la mer tous voyageurs
Menoient avec eux en voyage
Singes et chiens de bateleurs.
Un navire en cet équipage
Non loin d'Athènes fit naufrage.
Sans les dauphins tout eût péri.
Cet animal est fort ami
De notre espèce : en son histoire
Pline le dit; il le faut croire.[1]
Il sauva donc tout ce qu'il put.
Même un Singe en cette occurrence,
Profitant de la ressemblance,
Lui pensa devoir son salut :
Un Dauphin le prit pour un homme,
Et sur son dos le fit asseoir
Si gravement qu'on eût cru voir
Ce chanteur que tant on renomme.[2]
Le Dauphin l'alloit mettre à bord,
Quand, par hasard, il lui demande :
« Êtes-vous d'Athènes la grande?
— Oui, dit l'autre; on m'y connoît fort :
S'il vous y survient quelque affaire,
Employez-moi; car mes parents
Y tiennent tous les premiers rangs :
Un mien cousin est juge maire. »
Le Dauphin dit : « Bien grand merci;
Et le Pirée a part aussi
A l'honneur de votre présence?
Vous le voyez souvent, je pense?
— Tous les jours : il est mon ami;
C'est une vieille connoissance. »
Notre magot prit, pour ce coup,
Le nom d'un port pour un nom d'homme.

De telles gens il est beaucoup
Qui prendroient Vaugirard pour Rome,[3]
Et qui, caquetants au plus dru,
Parlent de tout, et n'ont rien vu.

Le Dauphin rit, tourne la tête,

THE APE AND THE DOLPHIN

They tell us that the Greeks, when they
Put out to sea in bygone day,
Would bring trained dogs and apes, and thus
Make voyages less tedious;
Whence the ensuing anecdote.
Off Athens' shores, just such a boat
Lay sinking: a catastrophe
But for the dolphins' help; that being
Whom Pliny, in his *History*—
And Pliny knows! No disagreeing!—
Shows to have much affinity
For us and ours. Well, as I said,
Without them all the crew were dead.
Instead, they saved all they were able;
Even an ape, whose human features
Misled one of those friendly creatures.
Quite like the dolphin in the fable
(Who snatched Arion from the sea,
Perched on his back), our friend, about
To take the monkey shoreward, out
Of danger, asks him, casually:
"Tell me, are you from Athens, sir?"
"Surely!" our simian *voyageur*
Replies. "Everyone knows me there.
If you have business anywhere
In Athens, see me! I'm your man!
If I can't help, my cousin can.
He runs the city." "Oh, I say!
Piraeus too?" "Piraeus? Why,
We're bosom comrades, he and I.
In fact, I see him every day."
"Piraeus? You and he... You're what?"
Bemused, the dolphin queries: "But..."

The ape, confusing man with place,
Was one of those unnumbered race
Who, never straying far from home,
Don't know their Vaugirard from Rome;
But who, undaunted, prate apace
On sights unseen.

       The dolphin turns,

Et le magot considéré,
Il s'aperçoit qu'il n'a tiré
Du fond des eaux rien qu'une bête.
Il l'y replonge, et va trouver
Quelque homme afin de le sauver.

Looks, eyes him, smiles, and finally learns
His man's a monkey, nothing more;
Tosses him back, still prattling, raving,
Into the sea; goes looking for
Some human creature worth the saving.

(IV, 7)

L'HOMME ET L'IDOLE DE BOIS

Certain Païen chez lui gardoit un Dieu de bois,
De ces dieux qui sont sourds, bien qu'ayants des oreilles :
Le Païen cependant s'en promettoit merveilles.
   Il lui coûtoit autant que trois :
   Ce n'étoient que vœux et qu'offrandes,
Sacrifices de bœufs couronnés de guirlandes.
   Jamais idole, quel qu'il fût,
   N'avoit eu cuisine si grasse,
Sans que pour tout ce culte à son hôte il échût
Succession, trésor, gain au jeu, nulle grâce.
Bien plus, si pour un sou d'orage en quelque endroit
   S'amassoit d'une ou d'autre sorte,
L'Homme en avoit sa part; et sa bourse en souffroit :
La pitance du Dieu n'en étoit pas moins forte.
A la fin, se fâchant de n'en obtenir rien,
Il vous prend un levier, met en pièces l'Idole,
Le trouve rempli d'or. « Quand je t'ai fait du bien,
M'as-tu valu, dit-il, seulement une obole?
Va, sors de mon logis, cherche d'autres autels.
   Tu ressembles aux naturels
   Malheureux, grossiers et stupides :
On n'en peut rien tirer qu'avecque le bâton,
Plus je te remplissois, plus mes mains étoient vides :
   J'ai bien fait de changer de ton. »

A pagan had an idol carved in wood;
    A god with ears, but one that stood
Deaf to his prayers, despite the gifts he bore him.
No matter: he was sure, one day, he could—
And would—repay the riches heaped before him:
Food, drink, fine beasts. . . Bulls crowned and garlanded. . .
    No god was ever so well fed.
The idol, though, continued to ignore him:
Never the merest trace of fortune's treasure.
What's more, whenever Fate dealt out displeasure—
Storm or whatever—he would reap his share.
    And though, in time, his purse grew bare,
Still, nonetheless, his god received full measure.
That is, until his patience reached its bounds:
    With iron bar he batters, pounds,
    Breaks the ungrateful god to bits.
    What does he find amid the rubble?
A pile of gold! "You wretch!" he cries. "For all my trouble
I never got one sou! Well, now we're quits!
You're just like Man and all his bloody lot;
You need the stick before you'll give one jot!
Go find some other worshipper to feed you.
Myself, the more I gave, the less I got.
It's good I saw the light. Now I don't need you."

(IV, 8)

43

The Jay Dressed in the Peacock's Feathers

LE GEAI PARÉ DES PLUMES DU PAON

Un Paon muoit : un Geai prit son plumage;
Puis après se l'accommoda;
Puis parmi d'autres Paons tout fier se panada,
Croyant être un beau personnage.
Quelqu'un le reconnut : il se vit bafoué,
Berné, sifflé, moqué, joué,
Et par Messieurs les Paons plumé d'étrange sorte;
Même vers ses pareils s'étant réfugié,
Il fut par eux mis à la porte.

Il est assez de geais à deux pieds comme lui,
Qui se parent souvent des dépouilles d'autrui,
Et que l'on nomme plagiaires.
Je m'en tais, et ne veux leur causer nul ennui :
Ce ne sont pas là mes affaires.

THE JAY DRESSED
IN THE PEACOCK'S FEATHERS

There was a peacock molting. Straightaway,
A jay put on the feathers he had shed
And, self-important, cocked a haughty head.
    Another peacock saw our jay—
Strutting among the flock in his disguise—
Who, forthwith, found himself unmasked, undone,
Hooted, jeered, jibed by each and everyone,
    And plucked in most uncommon wise.
Back home, his fellow jays no less despised him,
    Scorned him, and promptly ostracized him.

One also sees—wherever one may turn—
The human jay: the shameless plagiarist.
    But let him be; I'll not insist.
    Surely that's none of my concern.

(IV, 9)

The Camel and the Floating Sticks

Le premier qui vit un Chameau
S'enfuit à cet objet nouveau;
Le second approcha; le troisième osa faire
Un licou pour le Dromadaire.
L'accoutumance ainsi nous rend tout familier :
Ce qui nous paroissoit terrible et singulier
S'apprivoise avec notre vue
Quand ce vient à la continue.
Et puisque nous voici tombés sur ce sujet,
On avoit mis des gens au guet,
Qui voyant sur les eaux de loin certain objet,
Ne purent s'empêcher de dire
Que c'étoit un puissant navire.
Quelques moments après, l'objet devint brûlot,
Et puis nacelle, et puis ballot,[1]
Enfin bâtons flottants sur l'onde.

J'en sais beaucoup de par le monde
A qui ceci conviendroit bien :
De loin, c'est quelque chose; et de près, ce n'est rien.

THE CAMEL AND THE FLOATING STICKS

No doubt the first to see a camel
Fled from the unfamiliar mammal.
The second dared draw near; the third, less wary,
Fitted a halter to the dromedary.
Things that first seem extraordinary
Little by little grow less so. And thus
What once was fierce and strange to us
In time becomes an everyday affair.
Which brings me to my tale. Sometime, somewhere,
Some sentinels at water's edge espied—
Out there, adrift upon the distant tide—
Something that one and all agreed
Must surely be a mighty ship indeed.
Next moment it was just a boat;
And then a skiff; then smaller still;
And smaller, smaller yet, until
They saw that it was just some sticks afloat.

Many there are, I fear, who share that lot:
They look impressive from afar; up close, they're not.

(IV, 10)

47

The Frog and the Rat

LA GRENOUILLE ET LE RAT

Tel, comme dit Merlin, cuide engeigner autrui,
      Qui souvent s'engeigne soi-même.
J'ai regret que ce mot soit trop vieux aujourd'hui :
Il m'a toujours semblé d'une énergie extrême.[1]
Mais afin d'en venir au dessein que j'ai pris,
Un Rat plein d'embonpoint, gras et des mieux nourris,
Et qui ne connoissoit l'avent ni le carême,
Sur le bord d'un marais égayoit ses esprits.
Une Grenouille approche, et lui dit en sa langue :
« Venez me voir chez moi; je vous ferai festin. »
      Messire Rat promit soudain :
Il n'étoit pas besoin de plus longue harangue.
Elle allégua pourtant les délices du bain,
La curiosité, le plaisir du voyage,
Cent raretés à voir le long du marécage :
Un jour il conteroit à ses petits-enfants
Les beautés de ces lieux, les mœurs des habitants,
Et le gouvernement de la chose publique
          Aquatique.
Un point, sans plus, tenoit le galand empêché :
Il nageoit quelque peu, mais il falloit de l'aide.
La Grenouille à cela trouve un très-bon remède :
Le Rat fut à son pied par la patte attaché;
      Un brin de jonc en fit l'affaire.
Dans le marais entrés, notre bonne commère
S'efforce de tirer son hôte au fond de l'eau,
Contre le droit des gens, contre la foi jurée;
Prétend qu'elle en fera gorge-chaude et curée;
C'étoit, à son avis, un excellent morceau.
Déjà dans son esprit la galande le croque.
Il atteste les Dieux; la perfide s'en moque :
Il résiste; elle tire. En ce combat nouveau,
Un Milan, qui dans l'air planoit, faisoit la ronde,
Voit d'en haut le pauvret se débattant sur l'onde.
Il fond dessus, l'enlève, et par même moyen
      La Grenouille et le lien.
      Tout en fut : tant et si bien,
      Que de cette double proie
      L'oiseau se donne au cœur joie,
      Ayant de cette façon
      A souper chair et poisson.[2]

Merlin it was who said: "Chicane, and be
    Chicaned in turn!" (A lovely word,
"Chicane." I wish it weren't so rarely heard
    These days. It always sounds to me
    So forceful, full of strength, compelling. . .)
At any rate, back to the tale I'm telling.
    Down by a swamp, fat and content,
A gluttonous rat—a heathen he, who knew
Nothing of Advent, even less of Lent!—
Was passing time in carefree merriment,
When lo!, a frog came croaking by. "Good day to you!
    Pardon me if I interrupt;
    But Sire, I think it's time you supped
Chez moi. Come, I'll prepare a festive celebration."
His Rodentship accepts the invitation.
No need to ask him twice. And yet, the frog
    Harangues him with her monologue:
Ah! What fine things he'll tell the future generation!
    How nice the water. . . All the sights to see. . .
The swamp. . . Its people. . . Their society. . .
The government of the *res publica*
        Aquatica. . .
"I'll go! I'll go!" One problem, though: the rat
Is no great swimmer. "Bah! No problem that!"
Replies the frog. So saying, she takes some straw,
    Tying it tightly round his paw
And round her foot. Then to the swamp! Once there,
    Our kind and generous *commère*
Tugs at her guest, trying her best to drag him under.
(Morality be damned!) And little wonder:
    Already in her mind she's sinking
Her eager teeth into his flanks, and thinking
    "How tasty!". . . Rat resists. . . Frog tugs. . .
Rat curses her, invokes the gods. . . Frog shrugs. . .
And on the struggle rages, till a hawk on high,
        Casting voracious eye
        Upon our rotund rat,
        Swoops down, sweeps up his prey—
        With frog attached!—whereat
        He bears the pair away
    To feast on dish of fish and meat.

La ruse la mieux ourdie
Peut nuire à son inventeur;
Et souvent la perfidie
Retourne sur son auteur.

Such are the wages of deceit.
Carefully though the trickster lay
His snare, it may take but a minute
To catch him in it.

(IV, 11)

Le Pot de fer proposa
Au Pot de terre un voyage.
Celui-ci s'en excusa,
Disant qu'il feroit que sage
De garder le coin du feu;
Car il lui falloit si peu,
Si peu, que la moindre chose
De son débris seroit cause :
Il n'en reviendroit morceau.
« Pour vous, dit-il, dont la peau
Est plus dure que la mienne,
Je ne vois rien qui vous tienne.
— Nous vous mettrons à couvert,
Repartit le Pot de fer :
Si quelque matière dure
Vous menace d'aventure,
Entre deux je passerai,
Et du coup vous sauverai. »
Cette offre le persuade.
Pot de fer son camarade
Se met droit à ses côtés.
Mes gens s'en vont à trois pieds,
Clopin-clopant comme ils peuvent,
L'un contre l'autre jetés
Au moindre hoquet qu'ils treuvent.
Le Pot de terre en souffre; il n'eut pas fait cent pas[1]
Que par son compagnon il fut mis en éclats,
Sans qu'il eût lieu de se plaindre.

Ne nous associons qu'avecque nos égaux,
Ou bien il nous faudra craindre
Le destin d'un de ces Pots.

THE EARTHEN POT AND THE IRON POT

Said iron pot to earthen pot:
    "Let's travel, you and I."
Said earthen pot: "I'd rather not,
    My friend, and this is why:
For somebody the likes of me
It's best to stay home peacefully,
Here by the fire. It doesn't take
More than a touch to make me break
To bits, a-crumble and a-shatter.
With you it's quite another matter:
Go where you like; your iron hide
Is tough enough." The pot replied:
"I understand why you object.
You fail to fancy, I suspect,
That I'll protect you, come what may.
Indeed, you'll be my *protégé:*
Should object hard and unforeseen
Come threaten you, I'll stand between."
These promises at length persuade
His fretful friend, who, unafraid,
Accepts his offer. Off they go—
Two pots together, forward ho!—
Waddling along three-footedly;
But as they clip-clop, fancy-free,
The earthen pot, with every stride,
Is jarred and jostled by the one beside.
In but a yard or two, our pot—
With little right to wonder "Why?" or "Wherefore?"—
Lies in a shattered heap.

      My advice, therefore:
Keep to your kind. Because, if not,
You too may get the fate he got.

                    (V, 2)

LE PETIT POISSON ET LE PÊCHEUR

Petit poisson deviendra grand,
Pourvu que Dieu lui prête vie;
Mais le lâcher en attendant,
Je tiens pour moi que c'est folie :
Car de le rattraper il n'est pas trop certain.

Un Carpeau, qui n'étoit encore que fretin,
Fut pris par un pêcheur au bord d'une rivière.
« Tout fait nombre, dit l'homme en voyant son butin;
Voilà commencement de chère et de festin :
Mettons-le en notre gibecière. »
Le pauvre Carpillon lui dit en sa manière :
« Que ferez-vous de moi? je ne saurois fournir
Au plus qu'une demi-bouchée.
Laissez-moi carpe devenir :
Je serai par vous repêchée;
Quelque gros partisan m'achètera bien cher :[1]
Au lieu qu'il vous en faut chercher
Peut-être encor cent de ma taille
Pour faire un plat : quel plat? croyez-moi, rien qui vaille.
— Rien qui vaille? Eh bien! soit, repartit le Pêcheur :
Poisson, mon bel ami, qui faites le prêcheur,
Vous irez dans la poêle; et vous avez beau dire,
Dès ce soir on vous fera frire. »

Un Tiens vaut, ce dit-on, mieux que deux Tu l'auras :[2]
L'un est sûr, l'autre ne l'est pas.

THE LITTLE FISH AND THE FISHERMAN

Though every little fish, God willing,
Surely, one day, will bigger grow,
Folly it is to let one go
Until he's fatter for the killing.
Later you well may try, and not be able,
To land him when he's fitter for the table.

Angling at river's edge, a fisherman
Captured a baby carp—so goes the fable—
Eyeing it for his frying pan.
"Not much," he thought, "but every little bit. . ."
Then, just as he was putting it
Into his sack, somehow the fish pipes up:
"Good sir, before you take me home to sup,
Look at me, pray! Think what you're doing.
Really, I'm hardly worth the chewing!
Please, spare me; let me grow. You'll catch me later
And sell me to some tax administrator.
Whereas, merely to make some paltry dish,
You'll need a hundred more like me."
The fisherman replies: "Pish tush, poor fish!
Preach all you want. I guarantee,
Tonight you're landing in the skillet.
You're small, but still you're big enough to fill it!"

A fish in hand is worth two in the sea:
The one you hold is caught; the others, free.

(V, 3)

55

LA MONTAGNE QUI ACCOUCHE

Une Montagne en mal d'enfant
Jetoit une clameur si haute,
Que chacun, au bruit accourant,
Crut qu'elle accoucheroit sans faute
D'une cité plus grosse que Paris :
Elle accoucha d'une Souris.
Quand je songe à cette fable,
Dont le récit est menteur
Et le sens est véritable,
Je me figure un auteur
Qui dit : « Je chanterai la guerre
Que firent les Titans au maître du tonnerre. »
C'est promettre beaucoup : mais qu'en sort-il souvent?
Du vent.

THE MOUNTAIN IN LABOR

A pregnant mountain, just about
To enter labor, bellows out,
And raises such a monstrous roar
That all who run to watch surmise
She'll bear a city more than Paris' size.
A mouse is what she bore.
When I conceive this fiction,
Empty of fact but full of sense,
It seems to me a true depiction
Of authors' vain grandiloquence.
They promise: "Ah, my lyre will sing
Of Titans' combat with the Thunder's king."
Fine words! And yet, what often comes to pass?
Just gas.

(V, 10)

The Hen with the Golden Eggs

LA POULE AUX ŒUFS D'OR

L'avarice perd tout en voulant tout gagner.
Je ne veux, pour le témoigner,
Que celui dont la Poule, à ce que dit la fable,[1]
Pondoit tous les jours un œuf d'or.
Il crut que dans son corps elle avoit un trésor :
Il la tua, l'ouvrit, et la trouva semblable
A celles dont les œufs ne lui rapportoient rien,
S'étant lui-même ôté le plus beau de son bien.

Belle leçon pour les gens chiches!
Pendant ces derniers temps, combien en a-t-on vus
Qui du soir au matin sont pauvres devenus,
Pour vouloir trop tôt être riches!

THE HEN WITH THE GOLDEN EGGS

Longing for more, we lose what good we've got.
Witness the fabled hen who, so we're told,
    Each morning laid an egg of gold.
Not satisfied, her master lost the lot:
    Sure that her innards housed a treasure,
He killed her, cut her up, only to find
That she was quite the same, measure for measure,
    As hens that laid the common kind.

This lesson, greedy folk, is opportune:
Today, how many a pauper do we see,
    Who owes his sudden poverty
To his desire to grow too rich, too soon!

(V, 13)

L'ÂNE PORTANT DES RELIQUES

Un Baudet chargé de reliques
S'imagina qu'on l'adoroit :
Dans ce penser il se carroit,
Recevant comme siens l'encens et les cantiques.
Quelqu'un vit l'erreur, et lui dit :
« Maître Baudet, ôtez-vous de l'esprit
Une vanité si folle.
Ce n'est pas vous, c'est l'idole,
A qui cet honneur se rend,
Et que la gloire en est due. »

D'un magistrat ignorant
C'est la robe qu'on salue.

THE ASS WITH A LOAD OF HOLY RELICS

A jackass carrying a reliquary
    Assumed the people's veneration
    Was meant for him, in adulation
    Of qualities extraordinary,
Until, at length, to disabuse him, someone said:
    "Sir Ass, I fear you misconstrue.
    Best be advised to rid your head
Of witless vanity, or be misled!
    They merely give the god his due.
They're honoring the idol, dolt, not you!"

A judge can be a lout and little more:
His robes—not he—are what we bow before.

                  (V, 14)

The Stag Who Sees Himself in the Water

LE CERF SE VOYANT DANS L'EAU

Dans le cristal d'une fontaine
Un Cerf se mirant autrefois
Louoit la beauté de son bois,
Et ne pouvoit qu'avecque peine
Souffrir ses jambes de fuseaux,
Dont il voyoit l'objet se perdre dans les eaux.
« Quelle proportion de mes pieds à ma tête?
Disoit-il en voyant leur ombre avec douleur :
Des taillis les plus hauts mon front atteint le faîte;
Mes pieds ne me font point d'honneur. »
Tout en parlant de la sorte,
Un limier le fait partir.
Il tâche à se garantir;
Dans les forêts il s'emporte.
Son bois, dommageable ornement,
L'arrêtant à chaque moment,
Nuit à l'office que lui rendent
Ses pieds, de qui ses jours dépendent.
Il se dédit alors, et maudit les présents
Que le Ciel lui fait tous les ans.

Nous faisons cas du beau, nous méprisons l'utile;
Et le beau souvent nous détruit.
Ce Cerf blâme ses pieds, qui le rendent agile;
Il estime un bois qui lui nuit.

THE STAG WHO SEES HIMSELF
IN THE WATER

A stag, by crystal-running brook—
Stopping to have himself a look
At his reflection—gazed, gave thanks
For antlers full and fair, but took
Great umbrage at his spindly shanks,
Whose image, ill rewarding his inspection,
Shimmered below. "Ah me! What imperfection!
Such difference, head to toe! My brow can touch
The topmost branches, but my hooves are much
    The worst that ever were!" As thus
He wailed his woe in accents dolorous,
    A hound came bounding. Stag, in fright,
    Trying to flee into the wood
        As best he could,
        Turned to take flight.
And though his hooves performed quite as they should,
His antlers, tangling in each bough and limb,
    Would prove to be the death of him.
Damning his yearly growth, the beast, resigned,
Suffered a rather sudden change of mind.

Like stag, who cursed his hooves though quick to bless
The antlers that, at length, were his undoing,
We mortals prize the beautiful, eschewing
What serves us better, and what harms us less.

(VI, 9)

63

LE SOLEIL ET LES GRENOUILLES

Aux noces d'un tyran tout le peuple en liesse
              Noyoit son souci dans les pots.
Ésope seul trouvoit que les gens étoient sots
              De témoigner tant d'allégresse.
« Le Soleil, disoit-il, eut dessein autrefois
              De songer à l'hyménée.
Aussitôt on ouït, d'une commune voix,
              Se plaindre de leur destinée
              Les citoyennes des étangs.
       « Que ferons-nous, s'il lui vient des enfants?
« Dirent-elles au Sort : un seul Soleil à peine
              « Se peut souffrir; une demi-douzaine
« Mettra la mer à sec et tous ses habitants.
« Adieu joncs et marais : notre race est détruite;
              « Bientôt on la verra réduite
       « A l'eau du Styx. » Pour un pauvre animal,
Grenouilles, à mon sens, ne raisonnoient pas mal.

THE SUN AND THE FROGS

When, long ago, a tyrant wed,
His subjects drowned their woe in joyous wine.
Aesop alone thought it was asinine
To make such show of jollity, and said:
        "The Sun once took it in his head
                To take himself a bride.
        But suddenly, from swamps and fens,
Arose the voices of their denizens,
                Who, all together, cried:
'O Destiny! What horrors will betide
If he has sons? One Sun we can withstand,
But half-a-dozen will dry up the land:
No waters but the Styx to dwell beside!
                Reeds, rushes, marsh, adieu!
                To put it quite precisely,
        Our race is dead—done, finished, through!'"
For frogs, I think they reasoned rather nicely.

(VI, 12)

L'OISELEUR, L'AUTOUR ET L'ALOUETTE

Les injustices des pervers
Servent souvent d'excuse aux nôtres.
Telle est la loi de l'univers :
Si tu veux qu'on t'épargne, épargne aussi les autres.

Un Manant au miroir prenoit des oisillons.
Le fantôme brillant attire une Alouette :
Aussitôt un Autour, planant sur les sillons,
        Descend des airs, fond, et se jette
Sur celle qui chantoit, quoique près du tombeau.
Elle avoit évité la perfide machine,
Lorsque, se rencontrant sous la main de l'oiseau,
        Elle sent son ongle maline.
Pendant qu'à la plumer l'Autour est occupé.
Lui-même sous les rets demeure enveloppé :
« Oiseleur, laisse-moi, dit-il en son langage;
        Je ne t'ai jamais fait de mal. »
L'Oiseleur repartit : « Ce petit animal
        T'en avoit-il fait davantage? »

THE BIRD-CATCHER, THE HAWK, AND THE LARK

We use another's evil to condone
    No less an evil of our own.
    This is the moral law: *to do*
To others as you would have done to you.

    Out trapping birds, a country boor
Attracts a lark, drawn to his mirror-lure.
Soaring above the field, a hawk swoops, caws,
Pounces. . . The lark, still singing, at the edge of doom,
    Avoids the trap but not, alas, the tomb:
    The hawk sinks vicious taloned claws
    Into his unsuspecting victim.
    No sooner has he plucked him, picked him
Featherless, than, in turn, he feels the net
    Closing about him. "Free me! Let
Me go!" he clamors in his tongue. "I've done
    No harm to you, now or before!"
    "That's true," the peasant answers. "None. . .
Tell me, that lark. . . Did he do you much more?"

                    (VI, 15)

The Dog Who Drops His Prey for Its Reflection

LE CHIEN QUI LÂCHE SA PROIE
POUR L'OMBRE

Chacun se trompe ici-bas :
On voit courir après l'ombre
Tant de fous, qu'on n'en sait pas
La plupart du temps le nombre.
Au Chien dont parle Ésope il faut les renvoyer.
Ce Chien, voyant sa proie en l'eau représentée,
La quitta pour l'image, et pensa se noyer.
La rivière devint tout d'un coup agitée;
A toute peine il regagna les bords,
Et n'eut ni l'ombre ni le corps.

THE DOG WHO DROPS HIS PREY
FOR ITS REFLECTION

To err is human. Here below,
Many the folk—or fools—who go
Chasing a shadow; more, indeed,
Than one can count. Best let them read
The tale about a dog that Aesop tells,
Who, by a stream, prey clutched between his teeth,
Eyes its reflection in the waves beneath,
Lunges, falls in. The water swirls and swells.
Near drowned, he struggles back to shore. But oh, the cost:
Shadow and substance both, alas, are lost.

(VI, 17)

LA DISCORDE

La déesse Discorde ayant brouillé les Dieux,
Et fait un grand procès là-haut pour une pomme,[1]
    On la fit déloger des Cieux.
    Chez l'animal qu'on appelle homme
    On la reçut à bras ouverts,
    Elle et Que-si-Que-non, son frère,
    Avecque Tien-et-Mien, son père.
Elle nous fit l'honneur en ce bas univers
    De préférer notre hémisphère
A celui des mortels qui nous sont opposés,
    Gens grossiers, peu civilisés,
Et qui, se mariant sans prêtre et sans notaire,
    De la Discorde n'ont que faire.
Pour la faire trouver aux lieux où le besoin
    Demandoit qu'elle fût présente,
    La Renommée avoit le soin
    De l'avertir; et l'autre, diligente,
Couroit vite aux débats et prévenoit la Paix,
Faisoit d'une étincelle un feu long à s'éteindre.
La Renommée enfin commença de se plaindre
    Que l'on ne lui trouvoit jamais
    De demeure fixe et certaine;
Bien souvent l'on perdoit, à la chercher, sa peine :
Il falloit donc qu'elle eût un séjour affecté,
Un séjour d'où l'on pût en toutes les familles
    L'envoyer à jour arrêté.
Comme il n'étoit alors aucun couvent de filles,
    On y trouva difficulté.
    L'auberge enfin de l'Hyménée
    Lui fut pour maison assinée.

DISCORD

The goddess Discord, having sown her strife
    Throughout Olympus' ranks—and all
    Over an apple, you recall—
    Was banished from their midst for life,
    And sent to live, instead, among
The animal called Man. The latter fairly hung
About her neck welcoming her, along with brother
(True-False by name) and father (Thine-and-Mine) as well.
Ah, what an honor that the goddess chose to dwell
    Here, in our hemisphere, and not the other—
    In every way our opposite—
    Peopled with savages and such,
    Who, marrying without the benefit
Of notary and priest, would surely not have much
    For her to do. Well, be that as it may. . .
With Rumor as her guide, the exiled castaway
    Roamed here and there, spreading her fame,
    Fanning the slightest angry spark to flame,
    And keeping Peace and Harmony at bay.
    But Rumor soon complained, calling attention
    To Discord's lack of fixed address;
    Because, when one had need of her dissension,
    The search was long, and could be limitless.
And so, at length, it was decided she should be
    Lodged in a permanent location, whence
    She could, at proper times, dispense
    Her services. But, seeing that we
    Hadn't invented convents yet, where she
    Would be well housed, she took up residence
    In Holy Matrimony's hostelry.

(VI, 20)

LA JEUNE VEUVE

La perte d'un époux ne va point sans soupirs;
On fait beaucoup de bruit; et puis on se console :
Sur les ailes du Temps la tristesse s'envole,
    Le Temps ramène les plaisirs.
    Entre la veuve d'une année
    Et la veuve d'une journée
La différence est grande; on ne croiroit jamais
    Que ce fût la même personne :
L'une fait fuir les gens, et l'autre a mille attraits.
Aux soupirs vrais ou faux celle-là s'abandonne;
C'est toujours même note et pareil entretien;
    On dit qu'on est inconsolable;
    On le dit, mais il n'en est rien,
    Comme on verra par cette fable,
    Ou plutôt par la vérité.

    L'époux d'une jeune beauté
Partoit pour l'autre monde. A ses côtés, sa femme
Lui crioit : « Attends-moi, je te suis; et mon âme,
Aussi bien que la tienne, est prête à s'envoler. »
    Le mari fait seul le voyage.
La belle avoit un père, homme prudent et sage;
    Il laissa le torrent couler.
    A la fin, pour la consoler :
« Ma fille, lui dit-il, c'est trop verser de larmes :
Qu'a besoin le défunt que vous noyiez vos charmes?
Puisqu'il est des vivants, ne songez plus aux morts.
    Je ne dis pas que tout à l'heure
    Une condition meilleure
    Change en des noces ces transports;
Mais, après certain temps, souffrez qu'on vous propose
Un époux beau, bien fait, jeune, et tout autre chose
    Que le défunt. — Ah! dit-elle aussitôt,
    Un cloître est l'époux qu'il me faut. »
Le père lui laissa digérer sa disgrâce.
    Un mois de la sorte se passe;
L'autre mois, on l'emploie à changer tous les jours
Quelque chose à l'habit, au linge, à la coiffure :
    Le deuil enfin sert de parure,
    En attendant d'autres atours;
    Toute la bande des Amours

When woman loses mate, how many a sigh!
The weeping and the wailing past all measure!
        But not for long. Time, winging by,
Bears off her grief and brings back worldly pleasure.
        Betwixt our widows of a day
And of a year, I fear the gap is great;
So great, in fact, that one would almost say
They're different folk. The ones, disconsolate,
Rebuff, repel; the others charm, attract.
        The former. . . Ah, how sad they act,
        All sighs—or so it seems—unable
Ever to stem their tears, promising never,
Never to laugh or love again. However.
Best not believe it! Rather read my fable—
        More fact than fancy, by the way!

The husband of a fair young lovely lay
Abed, about to fly to his reward.
Close by his side, the wife cried, begged, implored:
        "Wait! Wait for me! I'm coming too!
My soul would waft aloft and leave with you!"
        But no. The husband left alone.
The lady's father is a prudent man.
He lets the widow weep and groan and moan
Until the torrent ends as it began.
Then, to console her: "Daughter dear," he said,
        "You've wept enough. Why should you let
        Grief drown your charms? The dead are dead,
        And have no need of tears. While yet
The living are alive, my love, forget
The past. I'll not suggest that by tomorrow
        Marriage must put an end to sorrow;
Still, in a while, I pray you let me find you
Someone to wed (and one who'll not remind you
Much of the first: young, handsome, well begot—
Everything, in a word, the first was not!)."
        "Ah," she replies, "in my sad state
None but the nunnery will be my mate!"
        Wisely he leaves her to her mourning.
One month goes by. But by the second, she
Has started adding frill and filigree

Revient au colombier; les jeux, les ris, la danse,
Ont aussi leur tour à la fin :
On se plonge soir et matin
Dans la fontaine de Jouvence.
Le père ne craint plus ce défunt tant chéri;
Mais comme il ne parloit de rien à notre belle :
« Où donc est le jeune mari
Que vous m'avez promis? » dit-elle.

To widow's weeds, costume and coif adorning.
In time, Love's band, in endless revelry,
      Come home to roost: song, dance, games, laughter. . .
Daughter awash in Youth, father hereafter
Worries no more about her buried past,
Yet holds his tongue. No talk of men. At last,
Our widow asks—all thought now turned to love:
"Papa, where's that young husband you were speaking of?"

                                           (VI, 21)

LE MAL MARIÉ

Que le bon soit toujours camarade du beau,
    Dès demain je chercherai femme;
Mais comme le divorce entre eux n'est pas nouveau,
Et que peu de beaux corps, hôtes d'une belle âme,
    Assemblent l'un et l'autre point,
Ne trouvez pas mauvais que je ne cherche point.
J'ai vu beaucoup d'hymens; aucuns d'eux ne me tentent :
Cependant des humains presque les quatre parts
S'exposent hardiment au plus grand des hasards;
Les quatre parts aussi des humains se repentent.[1]
J'en vais alléguer un qui, s'étant repenti,
    Ne put trouver d'autre parti
    Que de renvoyer son épouse,
    Querelleuse, avare, et jalouse.
Rien ne la contentoit, rien n'étoit comme il faut :
On se levoit trop tard, on se couchoit trop tôt;
Puis du blanc, puis du noir, puis encore autre chose.
Les valets enrageoient; l'époux étoit à bout :
« Monsieur ne songe à rien, Monsieur dépense tout,
    Monsieur court, Monsieur se repose. »
    Elle en dit tant, que Monsieur, à la fin,
    Lassé d'entendre un tel lutin,
    Vous la renvoie à la campagne
    Chez ses parents. La voilà donc compagne
De certaines Philis qui gardent les dindons
    Avec les gardeurs de cochons.
Au bout de quelque temps, qu'on la crut adoucie,
Le mari la reprend. « Eh bien! qu'avez-vous fait?
    Comment passiez-vous votre vie?
L'innocence des champs est-elle votre fait?
    — Assez, dit-elle; mais ma peine
Étoit de voir les gens plus paresseux qu'ici :
    Ils n'ont des troupeaux nul souci.
Je leur savois bien dire, et m'attirois la haine
    De tous ces gens si peu soigneux.
— Eh! Madame, reprit son époux tout à l'heure,
    Si votre esprit est si hargneux,
    Que le monde qui ne demeure
Qu'un moment avec vous et ne revient qu'au soir
    Est déjà lassé de vous voir,
Que feront des valets qui toute la journée

If it were true that, in this life,
Goodness and beauty travel hand in glove,
Tomorrow I would find myself a wife.
　　In truth, there's precious little love
Between the two, nor has there ever been.
Thus, if among the people feminine
　　Beautiful souls in bodies fair
　　Are altogether far too rare,
　　Don't be surprised if I eschew them:
Too many men I've seen whose wives undo them.
Marriage holds little charm for me; and yet, it
Tempts most of mankind, although most regret it.
　　To prove my point: a tale is told
　　About a certain gentleman
　　Who, married to a harridan—
　　A jealous, penny-pinching scold—
And harried by her carpings unrelenting,
　　Found himself all too soon repenting.
For her, do what one would, nothing was right.
Awake too soon... To bed too late... And how...? And who...?
And here's a how-de-do!... And black was white,
　　And white was black!... At length, the shrew
Exasperates the help, and husband too.
Fed up with insult and recrimination
("Monsieur does thus... Monsieur does so... Monsieur
Does this and that..."), Monsieur has quite enough of her,
　　And sends her on a long vacation,
Back to the country and her kin, among
Goosegirls and swineherds of a gentler tongue
　　And milder mien. In time, when she
Is thought to be less cross and crochety,
　　He brings her home. "I trust you spent
A pleasant time," says he, "in rustic sport,
　　Tasting the joys of innocent,
　　Bucolic life." The wife's retort:
"Oh, quite! Save for the fact that people there
Are even lazier than here! 'Shame! Shame!' I said,
'You let your flocks go roaming everywhere!'
　　But did they care? Oh no! Instead,
　　They said I was a meddlesome
Old crank!" "Ah so, madame... If you offend

Vous verront contre eux déchaînée?
Et que pourra faire un époux
Que vous voulez qui soit jour et nuit avec vous?
Retournez au village : adieu. Si, de ma vie,
Je vous rappelle et qu'il m'en prenne envie,
Puissé-je chez les morts avoir pour mes péchés
Deux femmes comme vous sans cesse à mes côtés! »

Mere strangers, who need only spend
An hour with you each day, think of the martyrdom
 Of servants and of spouse—days, nights on end!
 Off to the country, wife! Again, farewell!
 And if I bring you back—or fancy to!—
 May I pay for my sins in endless hell,
 With two wives, woman—both of them like you!"

(VII, 2)

Les Levantins en leur légende[1]
Disent qu'un certain Rat, las des soins d'ici-bas,
Dans un fromage de Hollande
Se retira loin du tracas.
La solitude étoit profonde,
S'étendant partout à la ronde.
Notre ermite nouveau subsistoit là dedans.
Il fit tant, de pieds et de dents,
Qu'en peu de jours il eut au fond de l'ermitage
Le vivre et le couvert : que faut-il davantage?
Il devint gros et gras : Dieu prodigue ses biens
A ceux qui font vœu d'être siens.
Un jour, au dévot personnage
Des députés du peuple rat
S'en vinrent demander quelque aumône légère :
Ils alloient en terre étrangère
Chercher quelque secours contre le peuple chat;
Ratopolis étoit bloquée :
On les avoit contraints de partir sans argent,
Attendu l'état indigent
De la république attaquée.
Ils demandoient fort peu, certains que le secours
Seroit prêt dans quatre ou cinq jours.
« Mes amis, dit le Solitaire,[2]
Les choses d'ici-bas ne me regardent plus :
En quoi peut un pauvre reclus
Vous assister? que peut-il faire
Que de prier le Ciel qu'il vous aide en ceci?
J'espère qu'il aura de vous quelque souci. »
Ayant parlé de cette sorte,
Le nouveau saint ferma sa porte.

Qui désignai-je, à votre avis,
Par ce Rat si peu secourable?
Un moine? Non, mais un dervis :
Je suppose qu'un moine est toujours charitable.

THE RAT WHO WITHDREW FROM THE WORLD

Putting aside all life's travail,
A certain rat—so goes a tale
    Of Eastern inspiration—
Fleeing the worldly drudgeries,
Took refuge in a fine Dutch cheese
To live in solitary contemplation,
Digging himself, by dint of claw and tooth,
    A peaceful habitat—
Bed, board, and all. For God, forsooth,
Rewards those folk—and lavishly, at that—
    Who dedicate their life and limb
    In perfect piety to Him.
    Now, one fine day, grown big and fat,
The pious soul receives an emissary—
Several, to be exact—from those of Rat persuasion,
Abroad on mission expeditionary
For help against an imminent invasion:
Ratopolis is under siege; the Cat—
    Cruel enemy—are everywhere!
    "Penniless, sir, we come with hat
In hand, to beg what little you can spare,
To save the Rat Republic; just enough until
Our foreign aid arrives, as presently it will."
    "Dear friends," replies the Solitaire,
    "Worldly concerns are mine no more.
Besides, what can you ask a holy hermit for?
    All I can do is pray for you, and then
    Pray yet again. And so I will. Amen."
Whereat our saintly interlocutor
    Turns on his heel and shuts the door.

Well now, I ask you, can you figure out
    Just whom my rat-tale is about?
A monk, you say? Nay, nay! One of those Turks—
    A dervish. Is there any doubt?
    Our monks do nothing but good works.

(VII, 3)

The Snake's Head and Tail

Le serpent a deux parties
Du genre humain ennemies,
Tête et Queue; et toutes deux
Ont acquis un nom fameux
Auprès des Parques cruelles :
Si bien qu'autrefois entre elles
Il survint de grands débats
Pour le pas.
La Tête avoit toujours marché devant la Queue.
La Queue au Ciel se plaignit,
Et lui dit :
« Je fais mainte et mainte lieue
Comme il plaît à celle-ci :
Croit-elle que toujours j'en veuille user ainsi?
Je suis son humble servante.
On m'a faite, Dieu merci,
Sa sœur et non sa suivante.
Toutes deux de même sang,
Traitez-nous de même sorte :
Aussi bien qu'elle je porte
Un poison prompt et puissant.
Enfin voilà ma requête :
C'est à vous de commander,
Qu'on me laisse précéder
A mon tour ma sœur la Tête.
Je la conduirai si bien
Qu'on ne se plaindra de rien. »
Le Ciel eut pour ces vœux une bonté cruelle.
Souvent sa complaisance a de méchants effets.
Il devroit être sourd aux aveugles souhaits.
Il ne le fut pas lors; et la guide nouvelle,
Qui ne voyoit, au grand jour,
Pas plus clair que dans un four,
Donnoit tantôt contre un marbre,
Contre un passant, contre un arbre :
Droit aux ondes du Styx elle mena sa sœur.

Malheureux les États tombés dans son erreur!

THE SNAKE'S HEAD AND TAIL

The snake has two extremities—
Her head and tail—and both of these
Are enemies of Man. On high,
The Fates view both with happy eye,
Content to see the harm they do.
Well, once upon a time, these two
Disputed over who, indeed,
        Should lead.
Since time began it always was the head
        That led;
And thus the tail discussed her case
Before the gods: "Must it be ever so?
Must she alone decide how far I go,
While I just follow on apace?
No, no! It's time that I resist her:
I'm not her servant, I'm her sister!
Thank heaven for that! Why must I be
The black sheep of the family?
My sting is no less venomous
Than hers. So, tell me, why the fuss?
Tail does as well as head can do.
I kill as fast, don't you forget it!
Treat us the same, and let me, too—
At last—be first. It's up to you.
Grant my request; you won't regret it.
I, too, was born to be a leader;
So let her follow, and let me precede her."
The gods, in cruel compliance, nod consent:
Often their kindness does more harm than good.
Vain wishes? Best ignore them, as they should.
Not this time, though. The tail, now newly bent
On leadership, but lost in blind bewilderment,
        Slithers—here, there—to no avail;
Goes bumping into walls, trees, men, and more;
And leads her sister to the Stygian shore.

Governments that act likewise, likewise fail:
Tails can't lead heads. And thereby hangs the tale.

        (VII, 17)

L'HOMME ET LA PUCE

Par des vœux importuns nous fatiguons les Dieux,
Souvent pour des sujets même indignes des hommes :
Il semble que le Ciel sur tous tant que nous sommes
Soit obligé d'avoir incessamment les yeux,
Et que le plus petit de la race mortelle,
A chaque pas qu'il fait, à chaque bagatelle,
Doive intriguer l'Olympe et tous ses citoyens,
Comme s'il s'agissoit des Grecs et des Troyens.

Un Sot par une Puce eut l'épaule mordue;
Dans les plis de ses draps elle alla se loger.
« Hercule, ce dit-il, tu devois bien purger
La terre de cette hydre au printemps revenue.
Que fais-tu, Jupiter, que du haut de la nue
Tu n'en perdes la race afin de me venger? »
Pour tuer une puce, il vouloit obliger
Ces Dieux à lui prêter leur foudre et leur massue.

THE MAN AND THE FLEA

How often, with our tiresome, irksome prayer,
We importune the gods! We seem to feel
They've little else to do but, eyes a-peel,
Pay heed to every mortal, everywhere.
Even the lowliest of the lot! As though
The merest jot and tittle here below
Ought move lofty Olympus quite as much
Or more than, say, the Trojan War or such!

A case in point: a flea, big as a louse,
Took up its lodging in a bumpkin's blouse
And bit his back. "You ought, O Hercules"—
So mused the sot—"rid earth of plagues like these,
This springtime scourge! And you, O Jove... I wonder
Why you don't purge their race in my defense!"
To kill one flea—O human impudence!—
He would enlist all heaven's might and thunder!

(VIII, 5)

85

The Hog, the Goat, and the Sheep

LE COCHON, LA CHÈVRE ET LE MOUTON

Une Chèvre, un Mouton, avec un Cochon gras,
Montés sur même char, s'en alloient à la foire.
Leur divertissement ne les y portoit pas;
On s'en alloit les vendre, à ce que dit l'histoire :
    Le Charton n'avoit pas dessein
    De les mener voir Tabarin.[1]
    Dom Pourceau crioit en chemin
Comme s'il avoit eu cent bouchers à ses trousses :
C'étoit une clameur à rendre les gens sourds.
Les autres animaux, créatures plus douces,
Bonnes gens, s'étonnoient qu'il criât au secours :
    Ils ne voyoient nul mal à craindre.
Le Charton dit au Porc : « Qu'as-tu tant à te plaindre?
Tu nous étourdis tous : que ne te tiens-tu coi?
Ces deux personnes-ci, plus honnêtes que toi,
Devroient t'apprendre à vivre, ou du moins à te taire :
Regarde ce Mouton; a-t-il dit un seul mot?
    Il est sage. — Il est un sot,
Repartit le Cochon : s'il savoit son affaire,
Il crieroit comme moi, du haut de son gosier;
    Et cette autre personne honnête
    Crieroit tout du haut de sa tête.
Ils pensent qu'on les veut seulement décharger,
La Chèvre de son lait, le Mouton de sa laine :
    Je ne sais pas s'ils ont raison;
    Mais quant à moi, qui ne suis bon
    Qu'à manger, ma mort est certaine.
    Adieu mon toit et ma maison. »

Dom Pourceau raisonnoit en subtil personnage :
Mais que lui servoit-il? Quand le mal est certain,
La plainte ni la peur ne changent le destin;
Et le moins prévoyant est toujours le plus sage.

THE HOG, THE GOAT, AND THE SHEEP

A sheep, a goat, a fatted hog were going
Together in one cart, off to the fair;
 But not to take their pleasure there,
Or watch the tricks that Tabarin was showing!
 The driver had but one intent.
According to the tale, he meant to find
A buyer for his beasts. As thus they went
Their way, poor Friar Swine cried, groaned, and whined
As if a hundred butchers chased behind—
Deafening clamor!—while the other two,
Quiet and well-behaved, surprised at his to-do,
 Were wondering at his shouts for help. "From what?
  No earthly harm can come to us!"
The driver asks him: "Why the bloody fuss?
We can't hear ourselves think! Please! Keep it shut!
Do like those other two. It's easy. Try it.
If they don't raise a rumpus, why should you?
 Look at the sheep. He's nice and quiet."
"Stupid, you mean! Believe me, if he knew
What he was in for, he'd be screaming too!
Likewise that other 'nice and quiet' so-and-so.
 Both of them think they only go
To leave their load: one, wool; the other, milk.
 That may be true. I wouldn't know.
 But as for me and all my ilk,
 No milk, no wool. . . Just meat! Ah, woe!
 Farewell, fair world! Home, hearth, good-bye!"

Our Friar judged his case with subtle eye;
But, truth to tell, that wouldn't change his state:
 Complain, lament, moan, perorate—
When pigs are going to fry, they're going to fry.
Wiser is he who tries to be blind to his fate.

         (VIII, 12)

LE RAT ET L'ÉLÉPHANT

Se croire un personnage est fort commun en France :
        On y fait l'homme d'importance,
        Et l'on n'est souvent qu'un bourgeois.
        C'est proprement le mal françois :
La sotte vanité nous est particulière.
Les Espagnols sont vains, mais d'une autre manière :
        Leur orgueil me semble, en un mot,
        Beaucoup plus fou, mais pas si sot.
        Donnons quelque image du nôtre,
        Qui sans doute en vaut bien un autre.

Un Rat des plus petits voyoit un Éléphant
Des plus gros, et railloit le marcher un peu lent
        De la bête de haut parage,
        Qui marchoit à gros équipage.
        Sur l'animal à triple étage
        Une sultane de renom,
        Son chien, son chat et sa guenon,
Son perroquet, sa vieille, et toute sa maison,
        S'en alloit en pèlerinage.
        Le Rat s'étonnoit que les gens
Fussent touchés de voir cette pesante masse :
« Comme si d'occuper ou plus ou moins de place
Nous rendoit, disoit-il, plus ou moins importants!
Mais qu'admirez-vous tant en lui, vous autres hommes?
Seroit-ce ce grand corps qui fait peur aux enfants?
Nous ne nous prisons pas, tout petits que nous sommes,
        D'un grain moins que les Éléphants. »
        Il en auroit dit davantage ;
        Mais le Chat, sortant de sa cage,
        Lui fit voir, en moins d'un instant,
        Qu'un Rat n'est pas un Éléphant.

THE RAT AND THE ELEPHANT

There is a trait abroad in France;
　　A fault most French; an illness: which is
　　Being too big to fit one's breeches.
How many burghers vainly pose and prance,
　　And do their little noble dance!
The Spaniards are no less vainglorious,
　　But in a different way from us;
　　　Their vanity is, in a word,
　　　Insane, while ours is just absurd.
Ours I can best portray in fable, thus:

　　　A rat of negligible size
Leered as a royal elephant loped past—
　　Accoutred in the finest wise—
And mocked the monster's lumbering gait, aghast
To see how all the folk, with awestruck eyes,
　　Admired the three-tiered beast, agape,
Watching it bear upon its back an entourage—
　　A pilgriming sultana, cat, dog, ape,
Parrot, duenna—all her vast ménage.
How could the populace admire that hulk!
　　"As if," thought he, "mere mass, mere bulk
Made some of us worth more than those with less.
Tell me, what quality do they possess
　　That makes you human beings delight?
Is it that giant form, that fills your young with fright?
　　The elephant is big, but we
Esteem ourselves not one jot less than he!"
　　He had a good deal more to say,
　　And would have done, had not the cat,
　　Uncaged, been quick to show him that
A rat's no elephant, think what he may.

(VIII, 15)

89

L'AVANTAGE DE LA SCIENCE

Entre deux Bourgeois d'une ville
S'émut jadis un différend :
L'un étoit pauvre, mais habile;
L'autre riche, mais ignorant.
Celui-ci sur son concurrent
Vouloit emporter l'avantage,
Prétendoit que tout homme sage
Étoit tenu de l'honorer.
C'étoit un homme sot; car pourquoi révérer
Des biens dépourvus de mérite?
La raison m'en semble petite.
« Mon ami, disoit-il souvent
Au savant,
Vous vous croyez considérable;
Mais, dites-moi, tenez-vous table?
Que sert à vos pareils de lire incessamment?
Ils sont toujours logés à la troisième chambre,
Vêtus au mois de juin comme au mois de décembre,
Ayant pour tout laquais leur ombre seulement.
La République a bien affaire
De gens qui ne dépensent rien!
Je ne sais d'homme nécessaire
Que celui dont le luxe épand beaucoup de bien.
Nous en usons, Dieu sait! notre plaisir occupe
L'artisan, le vendeur, celui qui fait la jupe,
Et celle qui la porte, et vous, qui dédiez
A Messieurs les gens de finance
De méchants livres bien payés. »[1]
Ces mots remplis d'impertinence
Eurent le sort qu'ils méritoient.
L'homme lettré se tut, il avoit trop à dire.
La guerre le vengea bien mieux qu'une satire.
Mars détruisit le lieu que nos gens habitoient :
L'un et l'autre quitta sa ville.
L'ignorant resta sans asile :
Il reçut partout des mépris;
L'autre reçut partout quelque faveur nouvelle :
Cela décida leur querelle.

Laissez dire les sots : le savoir a son prix.

THE VALUE OF KNOWLEDGE

Betwixt two burghers there arose
A row. One, quick of wit, was poor;
The other, rich, but much the boor.
The latter, twitting, clucks and crows:
Surely his bookish rival owes
The likes of him respect, and should—
If he, indeed, had any sense—
Pay homage to his opulence.
("Sense"? Hardly! Rather say "foolhardihood!"
For why revere mere wealth without
Real worth? It's meaningless.) "So, brother,"
Brashly the lout would taunt and flout
The other;
Doubtless you think yourself my better; but
How often do you have your friends to dinner?
What good are books? Will reading fill their gut?
The wretches just grow poorer, thinner;
Up in their garrets, garbed all year the same;
No servants but their shadows! Fie! For shame!
The body politic has little use
For those who never buy. Wealth and excess—
Luxury, in a word—produce
The greatest deal of human happiness.
Our pleasures set the wheel a-turning:
Earning and spending; spending, earning.
Each of us, Heaven knows, must play his part:
Spinners and seamsters, fancy beaus and belles
Who buy the finery the merchant sells;
And even you, who with your useless art,
Toady to patrons ever quick to pay."
Our bookman doesn't deign respond:
There's much too much that he might say.
But still, revenge is his, and far beyond
Mere satire's meager means. For war breaks out,
And Mars wreaks havoc round about.
Homeless, our vagabonds must beg their bread.
Scorned everywhere, the boor meets glare and glower;
Welcomed, the wit is plied with board and bed.

So ends their quarrel. Fools take heed: knowledge is power!

(VIII, 19)

LE GLAND ET LA CITROUILLE

Dieu fait bien ce qu'il fait. Sans en chercher la preuve
En tout cet univers, et l'aller parcourant,
      Dans les citrouilles je la treuve.
      Un Villageois, considérant
Combien ce fruit est gros et sa tige menue :
« A quoi songeoit, dit-il, l'auteur de tout cela?
Il a bien mal placé cette citrouille-là!
      Hé parbleu! je l'aurois pendue
      A l'un des chênes que voilà;
      C'eût été justement l'affaire :
      Tel fruit, tel arbre, pour bien faire.
C'est dommage, Garo, que tu n'es point entré
Au conseil de celui que prêche ton curé :
Tout en eût été mieux; car pourquoi, par exemple,
Le Gland, qui n'est pas gros comme mon petit doigt,
      Ne pend-il pas en cet endroit?
      Dieu s'est mépris : plus je contemple
Ces fruits ainsi placés, plus il semble à Garo
      Que l'on a fait un quiproquo. »
Cette réflexion embarrassant notre homme :
« On ne dort point, dit-il, quand on a tant d'esprit. »
Sous un chêne aussitôt il va prendre son somme.
Un Gland tombe : le nez du dormeur en pâtit.
Il s'éveille; et, portant la main sur son visage,
Il trouve encor le Gland pris au poil du menton.
Son nez meurtri le force à changer de langage.
« Oh! oh! dit-il, je saigne! et que seroit-ce donc
S'il fût tombé de l'arbre une masse plus lourde,
      Et que ce Gland eût été gourde?
Dieu ne l'a pas voulu : sans doute il eut raison;
      J'en vois bien à présent la cause. »
      En louant Dieu de toute chose,
      Garo retourne à la maison.

THE ACORN AND THE PUMPKIN

The Lord knows best what He's about.
No need to search for proof throughout
The universe. Look at the pumpkin.
It gives us all the proof we need. To wit:
The story of a village bumpkin—
Garo by name—who found one, gazed at it,
And wondered how so huge a fruit could be
Hung from so slight a stem: "It doesn't fit!
God's done it wrong! If He'd asked me,
He'd hang them from those oaks. Big fruit, big tree.
Too bad someone so smart and strong—
At least that's what the vicar's always saying
With all his preaching and his praying—
Didn't have me to help His work along!
I'd hang the acorn from this vine instead. . .
No bigger than my nail. . . It's like I said:
God's got things backwards. It's all wrong. . .
Well, after all that weighty thought I'd best
Take me a nap. We thinkers need our rest."
No sooner said than done. Beneath an oak
Our Garo laid his head in sweet repose.
Next moment, though, he painfully awoke:
An acorn, falling, hit him on the nose.
Rubbing his face, feeling his bruises,
He finds it still entangled in his beard.
"A bloody nose from this?" he muses.
"I must say, things aren't quite what they appeared.
My goodness, if this little nut
Had been a pumpkin or a squash, then what?
God knows His business after all, no question!
It's time I changed my tune!" With that suggestion,
Garo goes home, singing the praise
Of God and of His wondrous ways.

(IX, 4)

93

The Kite and the Nightingale

LE MILAN ET LE ROSSIGNOL

Après que le Milan, manifeste voleur,
Eut répandu l'alarme en tout le voisinage,
Et fait crier sur lui les enfants du village,
Un Rossignol tomba dans ses mains par malheur.
Le héraut du printemps lui demande la vie.
« Aussi bien que manger en qui n'a que le son?
        Écoutez plutôt ma chanson :
Je vous raconterai Térée et son envie.[1]
— Qui, Térée? est-ce un mets propre pour les milans?
— Non pas; c'étoit un roi dont les feux violents
Me firent ressentir leur ardeur criminelle.
Je m'en vais vous en dire une chanson si belle
Qu'elle vous ravira : mon chant plaît à chacun. »
        Le Milan alors lui réplique :
Vraiment, nous voici bien, lorsque je suis à jeun,
        Tu me viens parler de musique.
— J'en parle bien aux rois. — Quand un roi te prendra,
        Tu peux lui conter ces merveilles.
        Pour un milan, il s'en rira :
        Ventre affamé n'a point d'oreilles. »[2]

THE KITE AND THE NIGHTINGALE

The kite—bird of rapacious race—
Leading the village youth a merry chase,
Spreading his terror round, had pounced upon
    Spring's nightingale, who, woebegone,
Pled for her life: "What can you want with me?
    All voice and precious little meat!
Listen, I'll sing my famous melody.
Everyone loves it; so will you. You'll see. . .
    About Tereus. . . Love. . . Deceit. . ."
"Tereus? Is that something good to eat?"
    "Eat? No! He was a prince, whose passion
    Burned me in most unseemly fashion!"
"Oh? And what's that to me?" the kite replies.
    "Who cares? Of all the foolish things. . . !
Here I am, starving, and you rhapsodize!
    Enough!" "But sir, I sing for kings!"
"Then save your fancy tales till you get caught
    By bloody royalty!" he screeches.
"We kites don't give your art a second thought:
A hungry belly has no use for speeches."

                             (IX, 18)

The Turtle and the Two Ducks

LA TORTUE ET LES DEUX CANARDS

Une Tortue étoit, à la tête légère,
Qui, lasse de son trou, voulut voir le pays.
Volontiers on fait cas d'une terre étrangère;
Volontiers gens boiteux haïssent le logis.
    Deux Canards, à qui la commère
    Communiqua ce beau dessein,
Lui dirent qu'ils avoient de quoi la satisfaire.
    « Voyez-vous ce large chemin?
Nous vous voiturerons, par l'air, en Amérique :
    Vous verrez mainte république,
Maint royaume, maint peuple; et vous profiterez
Des différentes mœurs que vous remarquerez.
Ulysse en fit autant. » On ne s'attendoit guère
    De voir Ulysse en cette affaire.
La Tortue écouta la proposition.
Marché fait, les Oiseaux forgent une machine
    Pour transporter la pèlerine.
Dans la gueule, en travers, on lui passe un bâton.
« Serrez bien, dirent-ils, gardez de lâcher prise. »
Puis chaque Canard prend ce bâton par un bout.
La Tortue enlevée, on s'étonne partout
    De voir aller en cette guise
    L'animal lent et sa maison,
Justement au milieu de l'un et l'autre Oison.[1]
« Miracle! crioit-on : venez voir dans les nues
    Passer la reine des tortues.
— La reine! vraiment oui : je la suis en effet;
Ne vous en moquez point. » Elle eût beaucoup mieux fait
De passer son chemin sans dire aucune chose;
Car, lâchant le bâton en desserrant les dents,
Elle tombe, elle crève aux pieds des regardants.
Son indiscrétion de sa perte fut cause.

Imprudence, babil, et sotte vanité,
    Et vaine curiosité,
    Ont ensemble étroit parentage.
    Ce sont enfants tous d'un lignage.

THE TURTLE AND THE TWO DUCKS

A turtle, none too quick of mind,
And tiring of her hole, was quite inclined
To roam the world and visit lands far-flung.
(A common wish, especially among
        The lame, or slow of limb, confined
        To lodgings that they come to hate,
Such as our tortoise friend.) At any rate,
Two ducks she prattled to of her ambition
Assured her they could bring it to fruition:
        "Our highway is the sky, and we
        Can take you where you've never been.
We'll fly you to America! You'll see
Kingdoms, republics, peoples never seen.
        Imagine what you'll learn. You'll be
Just like Ulysses, traveling far and near."
(Ulysses? Who would think to find him here!)
        No sooner does she answer "Yes!"
        Than, there and then, the ducks prepare
        Their transport for our pilgrimess—
A simple stick. Each bites one end: "Now, there!"
They say. "You bite the middle." She complies.
        The ducks advise: "Hold tight! Take care!"
        And up they rise, high in the air,
        Much to the wonder and surprise
Of those below, who see her, house and all,
Hanging between two ducks! "Come look!" they call.
"A miracle! The Turtle Queen is flying
Heavenward!" "Queen!" she boasts. "There's no denying. . ."
Those words would be her last. Poor fool! She should
        Have kept her big mouth shut! Instead,
She opened it, and now it's shut for good,
As she lies—dashed to pieces—proud, but dead.

A babbling tongue, vain curiosity,
        And witlessness: one family!
        All of a kind, all kith and kin—
And all of them, in time, will do you in.

(X, 2)

The Lioness and the She-Bear

LA LIONNE ET L'OURSE

Mère Lionne avoit perdu son fan :
Un chasseur l'avoit pris. La pauvre infortunée
     Poussoit un tel rugissement
Que toute la forêt étoit importunée.
     La nuit ni son obscurité,
     Son silence et ses autres charmes,
De la reine des bois n'arrêtoit les vacarmes :
Nul animal n'étoit du sommeil visité.
     L'Ourse enfin lui dit : « Ma commère,
     Un mot sans plus : tous les enfants
     Qui sont passés entre vos dents
     N'avoient-ils ni père ni mère?
     — Ils en avoient. — S'il est ainsi,
Et qu'aucun de leur mort n'ait nos têtes rompues,
     Si tant de mères se sont tues,
     Que ne vous taisez-vous aussi?
     — Moi, me taire! moi, malheureuse?
Ah! j'ai perdu mon fils! Il me faudra traîner
     Une vieillesse douloureuse!
— Dites-moi, qui vous force à vous y condamner?
— Hélas! c'est le Destin qui me hait. » Ces paroles
Ont été de tout temps en la bouche de tous.

Misérables humains, ceci s'adresse à vous.
Je n'entends résonner que des plaintes frivoles.
Quiconque, en pareil cas, se croit haï des Cieux,
Qu'il considère Hécube, il rendra grâce aux Dieux.[1]

THE LIONESS AND THE SHE-BEAR

A mother lioness whose cub had been
Snatched from her den—a hunter was the thief—
    Stood roaring, groaning out her grief,
    Raising such an unholy din
Over the silence and the dark of night,
Despite the woodland's charms, that all the beasts therein
    Lay wide awake, try though they might
To fall asleep. At length the she-bear, in their plight,
    Decides to help. Approaching, chin to chin,
      "Tell me, madame," she asks, "those others. . .
Every whelp your claws and jaws did in. . .
      Didn't they all have fathers, mothers?"
"Certainly!" "Well, if they could hold their tongue
Whenever you were wont to kill their young,
    Then tell me, if it please you, why
Won't you be good enough at least to try!"
"What? Me? Be still?" thunders the beast, in anguish.
    "Still? When I've lost my only son?
    Bereft of all my hope. . . Undone. . .
    Old and abandoned, left to languish. . . "
"Whose fault, madame?" "Whose? Fate's! She loathes my very name!"
    Ah yes! It's Fate who always takes the blame.

      Poor mortals, you who blithely go
Charging the heavens with your every woe:
Consider Hecuba and all her sorry lot,
    Then thank those gods instead for what you're not!

(X, 12)

The Lion

LE LION

Sultan Léopard autrefois
Eut, ce dit-on, par mainte aubaine,
Force bœufs dans ses prés, force cerfs dans ses bois,
Force moutons parmi la plaine.
Il naquit un Lion dans la forêt prochaine.
Après les compliments et d'une et d'autre part,
Comme entre grands il se pratique,
Le sultan fit venir son vizir le Renard,
Vieux routier, et bon politique.
« Tu crains, ce lui dit-il, Lionceau mon voisin;
Son père est mort; que peut-il faire?
Plains plutôt le pauvre orphelin.
Il a chez lui plus d'une affaire,
Et devra beaucoup au Destin
S'il garde ce qu'il a, sans tenter de conquête. »
Le Renard dit, branlant la tête :
« Tels orphelins, Seigneur, ne me font point pitié;
Il faut de celui-ci conserver l'amitié,
Ou s'efforcer de le détruire
Avant que la griffe et la dent
Lui soit crue, et qu'il soit en état de nous nuire.
N'y perdez pas un seul moment.
J'ai fait son horoscope : il croîtra par la guerre;
Ce sera le meilleur Lion
Pour ses amis, qui soit sur terre :
Tâchez donc d'en être; sinon
Tâchez de l'affoiblir. » La harangue fut vaine.
Le Sultan dormoit lors; et dedans son domaine
Chacun dormoit aussi, bêtes, gens : tant qu'enfin
Le Lionceau devient vrai Lion. Le tocsin
Sonne aussitôt sur lui; l'alarme se promène
De toutes parts; et le Vizir,
Consulté là-dessus, dit avec un soupir :
« Pourquoi l'irritez-vous? La chose est sans remède.
En vain nous appelons mille gens à notre aide :
Plus ils sont, plus il coûte; et je ne les tiens bons
Qu'à manger leur part des moutons.
Apaisez le Lion : seul il passe en puissance
Ce monde d'alliés vivants sur notre bien.
Le Lion en a trois qui ne lui coûtent rien,
Son courage, sa force, avec sa vigilance.

THE LION

His Highness, Sultan Leopard, had—
With luck, they say—amassed a myriad
    Of subjects: many a sheep, and stag, and bull;
      Pastures, and woods, and meadows full.
One day a lion cub was born next door,
In neighboring realm. Once all the celebrations
      And *de rigueur* congratulations
Had run their course, the Sultan, sending for
      The wily fox, his Grand Vizier—
Cunning politico and old campaigner—
      Told him: "My friend, I know you fear
That newborn prince. But nothing could be plainer:
      He's not a threat. His father's dead,
Poor orphan! We should pity him instead!
He'll have his paws full with his own concerns.
If he can just hold on to what he's got,
      He'll thank his lucky stars, and not
Have time to plot new conquests." "Sire, one learns
      Politically," the fox replied
      With shake of head and accent snide,
"Whom not to waste one's pity on! You should
Do one of two things: either be his good
And faithful friend, or kill him now. Because,
      Once he has grown his teeth and claws,
      We're done for! That's the end! I've cast
His horoscope: his signs all point to war.
      No peril that he'll shrink before;
No foe more fierce, no friend more staunch and fast!
      So, you decide: friendship or death!"
      The Grand Vizier wasted his breath.
The Sultan was asleep; sleeping as well
Were all his subjects, while the young cub grew
      To lionhood, as cubs will do.
      And when he did. . . Too late! Ah, then
The tocsin peeled the country round! But when
The Sultan called the Grand Vizier, the latter,
      Sighing, complained: "What does it matter
How many a fine alliance we can muster!
      They'll come in droves, all bluff and bluster—
And just devour their share of sheep!—while he
      Has three allies, and only three:

Jetez-lui promptement sous la griffe un mouton;
S'il n'en est pas content, jetez-en davantage :
Joignez-y quelque bœuf; choisissez, pour ce don,
     Tout le plus gras du pâturage.
Sauvez le reste ainsi. » Ce conseil ne plut pas.
     Il en prit mal; et force États
     Voisins du Sultan en pâtirent :
     Nul n'y gagna, tous y perdirent.
     Quoi que fît ce monde ennemi,
     Celui qu'ils craignoient fut le maître.
Proposez-vous d'avoir le Lion pour ami,
     Si vous voulez le laisser craître.

His vigilance, his courage, and his strength.
Appease him, Sire... Some modest sacrifice...
A few fine lambs; a bull or two. The price
Is worth it if we save the rest." At length,
The Sultan spurned the Grand Vizier's advice.
　　His state, and neighbor states as well,
　　Brothers-in-battle, promptly fell
Before the lion. Struggle as they might,
His strength was more than all their might could quell.
　　The Grand Vizier, I fear, was right:
Unless you nip the lion in the bud,
Prepare to be his friend or shed your blood.

　　　　　　　　　　　　　　(XI, 1)

The Old Cat and the Young Mouse

LE VIEUX CHAT ET LA JEUNE SOURIS[1]

Une jeune Souris, de peu d'expérience,
Crut fléchir un vieux Chat, implorant sa clémence,
Et payant de raisons le Raminagrobis.[2]
  « Laissez-moi vivre : une souris
  De ma taille et de ma dépense
  Est-elle à charge en ce logis?
  Affamerois-je, à votre avis,
  L'hôte et l'hôtesse, et tout leur monde?
  D'un grain de blé je me nourris :
  Une noix me rend toute ronde.
A présent je suis maigre; attendez quelque temps.
Réservez ce repas à Messieurs vos enfants. »
Ainsi parloit au Chat la Souris attrapée.
  L'autre lui dit : « Tu t'es trompée :
Est-ce à moi que l'on tient de semblables discours :
Tu gagnerois autant de parler à des sourds.
Chat, et vieux, pardonner! cela n'arrive guères.
  Selon ces lois, descends là-bas,
  Meurs, et va-t'en, tout de ce pas,
  Haranguer les Sœurs filandières :
Mes enfants trouveront assez d'autres repas. »
  Il tint parole.

    Et pour ma fable
Voici le sens moral qui peut y convenir :
La jeunesse se flatte, et croit tout obtenir;
  La vieillesse est impitoyable.

THE OLD CAT AND THE YOUNG MOUSE

A mouse—young, inexperienced—
Thought he could pit his wit against
A wise old cat, Raminagrobis' kin.
    "Mercy, I pray," the mite commenced,
    Pleading his case to save his skin.
    "Mouse that I am, it must be clear
    I make but little difference here.
Surely my hosts—Madame, Monsieur, *et al.* —
    Won't starve for what I eat, indeed!
    A grain of wheat is all I need;
Why, with a nut I'd be a butterball!
    Besides, sir, I'm still much too small.
Save me to feed your children when I'm grown."
Replied the cat in condescending tone:
"You might as well be talking to the wall!
    My, how you err! To ask a cat
To spare you! And a wise, old one at that!
    You must think I'm a dunderhead!
Well, you can go harangue the Fates on high.
Children indeed! Don't worry, they'll be fed.
    Now, rules are rules: come down and die."
And so he did. *Requiescat!*

        In brief,
The moral of the tale I've been presenting?
Youth, sure it must prevail, must come to grief:
    Old age is cold and unrelenting.

(XII, 5)

The Sick Stag

LE CERF MALADE

En pays pleins de cerfs, un Cerf tomba malade.
Incontinent maint camarade
Accourt à son grabat le voir, le secourir,
Le consoler du moins : multitude importune.
« Eh! Messieurs, laissez-moi mourir :
Permettez qu'en forme commune
La Parque m'expédie; et finissez vos pleurs. »
Point du tout : les consolateurs
De ce triste devoir tout au long s'acquittèrent,
Quand il plut à Dieu s'en allèrent :
Ce ne fut pas sans boire un coup,
C'est-à-dire sans prendre un droit de pâturage.
Tout se mit à brouter les bois du voisinage.
La pitance du Cerf en déchut de beaucoup.
Il ne trouva plus rien à frire :
D'un mal il tomba dans un pire,
Et se vit réduit à la fin
A jeûner et mourir de faim.

Il en coûte à qui vous réclame,
Médecins du corps et de l'âme!
O temps! ô mœurs! j'ai beau crier,
Tout le monde se fait payer.

THE SICK STAG

Off in a land where stags abounded, one
    Fell ill. His friends came gathering round him,
Hoping to help; but soon he's overrun:
Stags by the score—each blessèd mother's son!—
Stags everywhere, to harass and to hound him.
    He begs: "Just let me die, I pray!
No tears! Let Fate do with me what she will. . . "
But no. When heaven pleased they went their way—
    And, heaven help us, not until!
    But first they drank a parting glass:
That is, encroaching on the stag's domain,
    They browsed it bare of bush and grass.
Now worse his woe, and mortal now his pain:
    Alas, our ailing quadruped,
    At length, lies starving. . . dying. . . dead.

    You doctors of the flesh and soul,
    You who should heal us, hale and whole,
How much you make us pay to live or die!
    I say my say, and sigh my sigh:
    "O tempora. . . " The old refrain. . .
    No matter; I cry out in vain!
    Everyone wants his piece of pie.

                       (XII, 6)

UN FOU ET UN SAGE

Certain Fou poursuivoit à coups de pierre un Sage.
Le Sage se retourne et lui dit : « Mon ami,
C'est fort bien fait à toi, reçois cet écu-ci :
Tu fatigues assez pour gagner davantage.
Toute peine, dit-on, est digne de loyer.
Vois cet homme qui passe, il a de quoi payer;
Adresse-lui tes dons, ils auront leur salaire. »
Amorcé par le gain, notre Fou s'en va faire
      Même insulte à l'autre bourgeois.
On ne le paya pas en argent cette fois.
Maint estafier accourt : on vous happe notre homme,
      On vous l'échine, on vous l'assomme.

      Auprès des rois il est de pareils fous :
      A vos dépens ils font rire le maître.
      Pour réprimer leur babil, irez-vous
      Les maltraiter? Vous n'êtes pas peut-être
      Assez puissant. Il faut les engager
      A s'adresser à qui peut se venger.

A FOOL AND A WISE MAN

A wise man out a-strolling finds behind him
A fool who takes delight in throwing stones.
Calm and unruffled, feigning not to mind him,
    The former, stopping, makes no bones,
But hands the fool a golden coin. "Good man,
Hard work like yours deserves reward! I can,
I fear, not give you what you're worth. But see
That burgher passing by? I'm sure that he
    Will pay you more than I. Go try him."
    The fool, whetted for gain, draws nigh him,
Pelts him as well. This time, no gold! Indeed,
    The burgher's men come running out,
And thrash the bumpkin soundly round about.

Kings, too, have fools of no less nasty breed:
They make their masters laugh at your expense,
But little can you do to make them rue it.
When such the case, it's only common sense
To let some other—stronger—victim do it.

                        (XII, 22)

L'AMOUR ET LA FOLIE

Tout est mystère dans l'Amour,
Ses flèches, son carquois, son flambeau, son enfance :
Ce n'est pas l'ouvrage d'un jour
Que d'épuiser cette science.
Je ne prétends donc point tout expliquer ici :
Mon but est seulement de dire, à ma manière,
Comment l'aveugle que voici
(C'est un dieu), comment, dis-je, il perdit la lumière,
Quelle suite eut ce mal, qui peut-être est un bien;
J'en fais juge un amant, et ne décide rien.

La Folie et l'Amour jouoient un jour ensemble :
Celui-ci n'étoit pas encor privé des yeux.
Une dispute vint : l'Amour veut qu'on assemble
Là-dessus le conseil des Dieux;
L'autre n'eut pas la patience;
Elle lui donne un coup si furieux,
Qu'il en perd la clarté des cieux.
Vénus en demande vengeance.
Femme et mère, il suffit pour juger de ses cris :
Les Dieux en furent étourdis,
Et Jupiter, et Némésis,
Et les Juges d'Enfer, enfin toute la bande.
Elle représenta l'énormité du cas :
« Son fils, sans un bâton, ne pouvoit faire un pas :
Nulle peine n'étoit pour ce crime assez grande :
Le dommage devoit être aussi réparé. »
Quand on eut bien considéré
L'intérêt du public, celui de la partie,
Le résultat enfin de la suprême cour
Fut de condamner la Folie
A servir de guide à l'Amour.

LOVE AND FOLLY

Love is the deepest mystery.
Cupid, that childish knave of knaves—
With quiver, arrows, torch—behaves
So darkly that, in truth, if we
Are wont to fathom him, I fear
We'll need not just a day, not just a year!
Thus let me say, before I start,
That's not at all my purpose here.
I only wish to use my humble art
To tell you how that godling, blind,
First came to lose his sight: a woesome ill,
But one that many a lover is inclined
To think a boon. Myself, I'm keeping still.

Folly and Love, one day at play together,
Had a dispute. The latter wondered whether
The Council of the Gods ought not be called.
Folly, incensed, punched, flailed away
And robbed the other of the light of day;
Whose mother, Venus, properly appalled—
Shrieking for vengeance, woman that she was—
Deafened the gods and won them to her cause:
Nemesis, Jove, Hell's judges too—
In short, the whole Olympian crew.
"No punishment is harsh enough," she pleaded;
"My son is now an invalid.
Do what you have to do!" The court acceded,
And so, indeed, do it they did:
In view of public weal and private woe,
They sentenced Folly evermore to go
Abroad with Love, whithersoever,
And be his constant guide, forever.

(XII, 14)

This conclusion, opening its endless perspective on the human condition, seemed like such an appropriate ending for my collection that I have taken the liberty of displacing the fable slightly from La Fontaine's intended order. My apologies for any offense to the punctilious purists among my readers.

NOTES

The Frog Who Would Grow as Big as the Ox

1. La Fontaine's last line has become proverbial. As for the whole of the final quatrain, a number of critics were to take him to task for unnecessarily appending self-evident morals to many of his fables—a point of view by no means universally shared. Jean-Jacques Rousseau especially—no lover of La Fontaine's moralizings—citing this fable, observes in a well-known passage from Book Four of his pedagogical treatise *Émile* (1762): "Si votre élève n'entend la fable qu'à l'aide de l'explication, soyez sûr qu'il ne l'entendra pas même ainsi" (ed. Michel Launay [Paris: Garnier-Flammarion, 1966], p. 323). For the present fable at any rate, not to mention all the rest, the reproach is unwarranted on literary grounds if no other. At least one of the several Aesopic originals (Phaedrus, I, 24) begins with a similar explanatory moral: "Inops, potentem dum vult imitari, perit. . . " ("When the poor man wants to ape the powerful, he comes to grief. . . ").

The Thieves and the Ass

1. The name "maître Aliboron," used here by La Fontaine to designate the ass, has a lengthy history. Derived from the hellebore (in Latin, *elleborum*), a powerful medicinal plant known since ancient times, the name came to be commonly used by medieval and Renaissance French writers—Rabelais among them—to indicate a pretentious charlatan. An etymological connection with the name of the Arabian mathematician-philosopher Al-Birouni has also been suggested. (See Jaqueline Picoche, *Nouveau Dictionnaire étymologique du français* [Paris: Hachette-Tchou, 1971], p. 18.)

The Cock and the Pearl

1. This fable is an example of La Fontaine's occasional device of turning the general to the concrete, in updated dress. The Aesopic model (Phaedrus, III, 12), widely reworked throughout the Middle Ages and beyond, makes no specific mention of manuscripts and booksellers. Other examples in the present collection will be self-evident.

The Fox and the Grapes

1. Gascons in France are known for their bluster and braggadocio, and Normans for their shrewdness, though neither quality is especially evident in La Fontaine's rendition of Aesop's celebrated fox.

The Ape and the Dolphin

1. La Fontaine's comment reflects the high esteem in which the literati of the Western world held Pliny the Elder's first-century *Historia naturalis,* from the Middle Ages through the end of the seventeenth century. His prestige began to wane only with the advent of more scientifically discriminating commentators.

2. According to legend, Arion, the Greek poet said to have flourished at the court of Corinth some seven centuries before Christ, was saved by a dolphin after jumping into the sea to escape from a band of thieving sailors. The tale is told by Herodotus (I, 23, 24) and by Pliny (IX, 8), among others. Arion is immortalized astronomically as a constellation representing the dolphin and the lyre.

3. Vaugirard, in La Fontaine's day, was a small village not yet incorporated into the city limits of Paris. The name was commonly used to suggest "the sticks," as in the proverbial *prendre Vaugirard pour Rome.* (See Regnier, *Œuvres de J. de la Fontaine,* I:293.)

The Camel and the Floating Sticks

1. The *brûlot* and *ballot* of the original, which I avoid translating literally, refer, respectively, to a fire-boat (i.e., a small craft used in the seventeenth and eighteenth centuries to set fire to enemy vessels) and a bundle of rags or the like.

The Frog and the Rat

1. La Fontaine's aphorism—with his typically chatty aside on the archaic verb *engeigner*—was proverbial. As for the "Merlin" referred to, not all commentators are in agreement. In all likelihood it is an allusion to the popular sixteenth-century collection of prophecies and legends anonymously attributed to King Arthur's famous sorcerer; though others have taken it to be an allusion to the work of the Italian macaronic poet Teofilo Folengo, whose poem *Baldus,* first published in 1517 under the

pseudonym of Merlin Coccaie (and republished several times thereafter), supposedly served as a prototype for Rabelais. La Fontaine's maxim in question is found both in the former and in at least some versions of the latter. (See Regnier, *Œuvres de J. de la Fontaine,* I:306–8.)

2. Although a lover of animals and a defender of their integrity against the Cartesians, who thought of them as mere mindless machines—his celebrated "Discours à Madame de la Sablière" in Book IX argues the point eloquently—La Fontaine would appear to be no zoologist, classifying the frog as a fish. (The misconception does not occur in the Aesopic original, drawn from the medieval *Life of Aesop* [see Regnier, *Œuvres de J. de la Fontaine,* I:52], though I cannot state with any certainty that it is not found in any of the subsequent versions of the same fable, with which La Fontaine may or may not have been acquainted.) More than likely, at any rate, he is thinking theologically here, rather than zoologically, the frog being permissible fare on fast days.

The Earthen Pot and the Iron Pot

1. Without being mathematical, I think it safe to assume that "cent pas," when traveled by a pot, is no great distance. Hence my translation.

The Little Fish and the Fisherman

1. In the sixteenth and seventeenth centuries, *partisan* was one of the common euphemisms for financier; or, more especially, tax collector: one who made a *parti,* or contract, with the king for that purpose.

2. The original "un 'tiens' vaut mieux que deux 'tu l'auras'" is a common and ancient proverb. The context makes my translation more appropriate than the usual English equivalent of "A bird in the hand. . ."

The Hen with the Golden Eggs

1. Some Aesopic antecedents identify the wonderful bird in question as a goose, more familiar to our ears than the present *poule.* (See, for example, no. 87 of the "Fabulae Graecae," in Ben Edwin Perry's *Aesopica*

[Urbana: University of Illinois Press, 1952], p. 355.) Others, like Babrius, 123—La Fontaine's probable model—refer merely to an *ornis,* "bird," though the Greek word often does refer specifically to the hen.

Discord

1. The reference is, of course, to the famous apple that Discord offered to "the most beautiful" of the goddesses assembled at the wedding feast of Thetis and Peleus. According to Greek legend, it was Paris who awarded it to Venus, thereby incurring the wrath of Juno and Minerva and precipitating their spiteful vengeance, resulting, eventually, in the fall of Troy.

The Man Who Married a Shrew

1. La Fontaine was not nearly as misogynistic as this introduction, and the two preceding fables, would imply, having enjoyed a number of female relationships, both platonic and romantic. His one marriage, however—to sixteen-year-old Marie Héricart—appears to have been arranged with an eye to her considerable dowry, and was marred almost from its beginning by constant misunderstandings. It resulted in a legal separation in 1658, twenty or so years before the present fable was published, lasting throughout the rest of his life. (La Fontaine's amours, especially from the time of his marriage on, have been sympathetically chronicled by twentieth-century fabulist Franc-Nohain [pseudonym of Maurice Legrand], in *La Vie amoureuse de Jean de La Fontaine* [Paris: Flammarion, 1928].)

The Rat Who Withdrew from the World

1. The religious context of this fable underscores the original meaning of the term *légende;* that is, a collection of moral precepts dating from the early days of the Church and eventually including lives of saints, martyrs, and other *legenda:* materials "to be read," for the edification of the pious. The alleged Eastern inspiration is probably a fiction invented by La Fontaine to render the dénouement more palatable. (See Regnier, *Œuvres de J. de la Fontaine,* II:106-7.)

2. One is easily tempted to see here a pointed allusion to the Solitaires of Port-Royal, the Jansenist religious community among whose most celebrated adepts had been the philosopher Pascal. Their ascetic

discipline was clearly at odds with La Fontaine's easygoing and almost libertine life-style; an antagonism expressed in works like his "Ballade sur Escobar" (1664), in which he explicitly criticizes the Jansenists for being spoilsports (". . . nous défendent en somme / Tous les plaisirs que l'on goûte ici-bas."). His flirtation with various projects of religious verse—among them the "Poème de la captivité de Saint-Malc" (1673), done at the urging of certain Port-Royalists some five years before publication of the present fable—without blunting the temptation to read anti-Jansenist sentiments into the allusion, points, rather, to La Fontaine's typical vacillation between the values of flesh and spirit, as well as to a good-natured willingness to lend his talents to a variety of endeavors.

The Hog, the Goat, and the Sheep

1. "Tabarin" was the pseudonym of a hugely popular Parisian mountebank and huckster of the 1620s, who worked in collaboration with the charlatan "Mondor"—also a pseudonym—selling unguents and potions on the Pont Neuf and Place Dauphine. His blatantly physical and verbal humor was a blend of medieval French farce tradition and the Italian *commedia dell'arte*, whose practitioners had been established on the Parisian theatrical scene since 1570. (See *Œuvres complètes de Tabarin, avec les rencontres, fantaisies et coq-à-l'âne facétieux du baron de Gratelard, et divers opuscules publiés séparément sous le nom ou à propos de Tabarin,* ed. Gustave Aventin [Auguste Veinant], 2 vols. [Paris: P. Jannet, 1858].) Tabarin's real name, in all likelihood, was Antoine Girard, though for a long time the man behind the mask was thought to be one Jean Salomon. (See Georges Mongrédien, "Bibliographie tabarinique," in *Bulletin du bibliophile,* 1928, pp. 358–68, 415–47.)

The Value of Knowledge

1. La Fontaine might appear, in this passage, to be an early proponent of the laissez-faire capitalistic theory that luxury is an important driving force in a healthy economy; the idea that was to underlie Bernard Mandeville's celebrated and controversial treatise on the social utility of selfishness, *The Fable of the Bees, or Private Vices, Publick Benefits* (1714). (It is probably only coincidental that Mandeville had also anonymously adapted a number of La Fontaine's fables into English, under the title *Some Fables After the Easie and Familiar Method of Monsieur de la Fontaine* [London, 1703], though unfortunately from the point of view of literary serendipity, the present fable is not among

them.) Voltaire would develop Mandeville's notion in his poem "Le Mondain" (1736)—singing the praises of luxury as "le superflu, chose très nécessaire..." (line 22)—as well as in subsequent writings. (See André Morize, *L'Apologie du luxe au XVIIIe siècle et "le Mondain" de Voltaire* [Paris: Didier, 1909].) Given La Fontaine's dénouement, however, it would be risky to attribute to him too serious or sympathetic an attitude toward the economic preachments of his wealthy burgher. (See Gustave Boissonade, *La Fontaine économiste* [Paris: Guillaumin, 1872], pp. 8–10.)

The Kite and the Nightingale

1. The tale that La Fontaine's nightingale offers to sing would be about Tereus, mythological king of Thrace, who seduced Philomela while married to her sister Procne. To keep the former from telling, he cut out her tongue; but she managed to transmit the news to the queen by weaving it into her embroidery. Procne took revenge by murdering Tereus's son and serving him up for supper. The king, enraged, tried to kill the two sisters, but the gods took pity and turned them into birds. (Sources differ as to which became the swallow and which the nightingale, though French tradition generally identifies the latter with Philomela.) Tereus himself was metamorphosed into the hawk, or, according to other accounts, into the much less fearsome hoopoe.

2. Although often credited with having done so, La Fontaine did not originate the pithy French proverb that concludes this fable. It is found, a century earlier, in Rabelais (*Pantagruel,* Fourth Book, chapter 63), and may well have predated even him. But the idea, at any rate, goes back to antiquity. Plutarch mentions that Cato the Censor, addressing the Roman citizenry in time of famine, assured them: "It is a hard thing (my Lords of Rome) to bring the belly by persuasion to reason, that hath no ears." (See Sir Thomas North's 1579 translation of Plutarch's *Lives of the Noble Grecians and Romans,* reprint ed., 8 vols. [New York: The Limited Edition Club, 1941], III:179.)

The Turtle and the Two Ducks

1. If the reader wonders how each of La Fontaine's ducks ("canards") could suddenly be transformed into a gosling ("oison"), he should be aware that others too have asked the same question. For the venerable lexicographer Littré, the poet was guilty of "une inexactitude de langage, malgré la parenté de l'oie et du canard." (See the entry on *oison* in É Littré, *Dictionnaire de la langue française,* 4 vols. and supplement

[Paris: Hachette, 1881–83], III:815.) Be that as it may, I have taken the liberty of not following La Fontaine in his pardonable "inexactitude."

The Lioness and the She-Bear

1. Hecuba's name has long been synonymous with overwhelming suffering. Wife of the Trojan king Priam, she was victim of numerous horrendous misfortunes after the fall of Troy, as portrayed by Euripides and other classical authors. Not the least, and the one to which La Fontaine is obviously referring, was the loss of most of her nineteen children; among them Paris, Troilus, Hector, Cassandra, and Polydorus.

The Old Cat and the Young Mouse

1. This fable was written as a "command performance" for Louis XIV's grandson, the young Duc de Bourgogne, for whom that title had been revived a few years before, in 1682. According to twenty-two lines of prefatory verse, it was composed at the request of the royal scion, "qui avoit demandé à M. de la Fontaine une fable qui fût nommée *le Chat et la Souris.*"

2. Raminagrobis, the name La Fontaine uses for his stuffy old cat, was borrowed—like a number of his proper names—from Rabelais (*Pantagruel,* Third Book, chapter 21), who gives it to the old poet—supposedly modeled after Guillaume Crétin—visited by Pantagruel and Panurge during their consultations on the advisability of the latter's marriage. The word came to be used throughout the Renaissance as an adjective meaning "pompous," "vain," and even gave rise to a verb, *raminagrobiser,* in a legal context, meaning "to pussyfoot like a lawyer"—no pun intended.

A Note on the Translator

NORMAN R. SHAPIRO is professor of Romance languages and literatures at Wesleyan University. His B.A., M.A., and Ph.D. are from Harvard University. He is recognized as an outstanding translator of French and has published extensively in this role. His books include *Four Farces by Georges Feydeau, The Comedy of Eros,* a number of novels, *Feydeau, First to Last,* and *Fables from Old French.* Many of his translations have appeared in journals and anthologies, and his theater translations are widely performed.

A Note on the Illustrator

ALAN JAMES ROBINSON, co-founder of Cheloniidae Press, is an award-winning printmaker, book designer, and sculptor. He has produced meticulously crafted editions of such works as Edgar Allan Poe's *The Black Cat* and *The Raven,* Mark Twain's *The Notorious Jumping Frog of Calaveras County,* and Thomas Browne's *Of Unicorne's Hornes.* His work has appeared or can be found in numerous private and public collections, including those of the New York Public Library and Yale, Princeton, and Harvard universities.